A HISTORY OF BOSTON

IN 50 ARTIFACTS

Joseph M. Bagley

A HISTORY

OF BOSTON

IN 50 ARTIFACTS

University Press of New England | Hanover and London

University Press of New England
www.upne.com
© 2016 Joseph M. Bagley
All rights reserved
Manufactured in the United States of America
Designed by Mindy Basinger Hill
Typeset in Adobe Jenson Pro

Library of Congress Cataloging-in-Publication Data

Names: Bagley, Joseph M., 1985–
Title: A history of Boston in 50 artifacts / Joseph M. Bagley.
Other titles: History of Boston in fifty artifacts
Description: Hanover: University Press of New England, 2016. | Includes bibliographical references and index.
Identifiers: LCCN 2015040339 | ISBN 9781611687828 (pbk.) | ISBN 9781611689648 (ebook)
Subjects: LCSH: Boston (Mass.)—Antiquities—Pictorial works. | Boston (Mass.)—History—Pictorial works. | Boston (Mass.)—Antiquities. | Boston (Mass.)—History. | Material culture—Massachusetts—Boston—History.
Classification: LCC F73.39 .B34 2016 | DDC 974.4/61—dc23
LC record available at http://lccn.loc.gov/2015040339

5   4   3   2

TO JEN

Contents

Preface

Near the fall of 2013, I was working in a historic carriage house in the Dorchester neighborhood of Boston restoring shutters from an 1806 house. To keep sane during the tedious work, I had an NPR podcast playing on the radio when I heard an introduction to the next story, the release of a new book by the British Museum, *A History of the World in 100 Objects* (MacGregor 2011). During the break that followed on the radio, I was thinking that it would be great if someone wrote a history of Boston based on artifacts from Boston archaeological sites. Then I realized that as city archaeologist, that person should probably be me, so I immediately started brainstorming artifacts to include, and that evening I was Googling "how to write a book proposal."

Less than two years previously, in December 2011, I became one of the luckiest living archaeologists when I was offered my dream job: the city archaeologist of Boston. I had grown up in Maine struggling to decide in high school what I wanted to do for the rest of my life. I knew what I didn't want: a job that I didn't love. I knew I loved science, but was more interested in the investigation and discovery aspects than the chemistry- or math-based sciences. I'm not sure what triggered the idea—either it was a TV show featuring an archaeological dig, or maybe it was one of the majors listed in a college brochure, but I started looking into archaeology as a career during my senior year of high school. The idea of being an archaeologist, making discoveries, and traveling made me more excited about my future life than anything else I was considering at the time.

A few very fortunate events followed. First, I was accepted into my first-choice college, Boston University (BU), which had its own independent archaeology degree program for undergraduates. It may have also been the only university that accepted me, but it was a perfect fit, regardless. Soon after getting accepted into BU, it dawned on me that what I saw on TV and online may not be reality for most archaeologists, so I started trying to track down digs in my home state of Maine that I could participate in during the summer before I left for school, just in case I hated it.

The Maine State Museum offered a one-week field program in Down East Maine on the Goddard site, a multicomponent Native site practically made of artifacts. While it was no Egypt or Peru, digging on the coast of Maine feet from the ocean with a view of Acadia National Park was, in my opinion, just as good, and I completely fell in love with archaeology.

Words cannot describe how much I enjoyed studying archaeology at BU: I met my wife, Jen, who is also an archaeologist; I made a ton of friends I still have today; and I got to live in a specialty dorm where only archaeology and classics majors were allowed. It was a full-immersion experience. Just before my first summer at BU, I begged the state archaeologist of Maine to let me volunteer for his office during the summer to get experience. He said yes, for some reason, and I spent the summer creating a digital map of all of the archaeological sites and surveys in Maine. The next three summers I was invited back, but this time as a paid field technician for the small cultural resource management (CRM) firm based out of the State Historic Preservation Office (SHPO). I showed up on my first day of CRM in western Maine at the age of eighteen wearing shorts and sandals, and I did not bring water. I have come a long way since then. I realized that a field school and CRM are very different things. I dug my first test pit (poorly), had to learn metric measurements, threw out a ton of clay tobacco pipe stems, thinking they were sticks (this was my first historic site), and shook my head as someone patiently attempted, without much success, to teach me the differences between creamware, pearlware, and whiteware. This crew did archaeological digs for development projects throughout the state, and I will be eternally grateful for the Maine crew's patience, encouragement, and near-constant stream of Monty Python and SNL skit quotes.

Toward the end of my time at BU, I reached the point where I had to take a field school as a requirement of the degree track. This was my opportunity to travel, but the financial reality of summer field schools became a reality, and I made the choice to have another summer of paid archaeological employment count toward my field school requirement. While this means I still have never done archaeology outside the United States (or the East Coast, for that matter), it did solidify my interests, passion, and commitment to local New England archaeology.

During my senior year at BU in 2006, I wrote a thesis on a Boston Native site (which includes artifacts 2 and 4 presented in this book). I was rejected from the only graduate program I applied to, frustratingly, but I found work as an intern at the Massachusetts Historic Commission working in their Technical Service Division, assisting their archaeological staff in their review of development projects. This review checks for potential impacts on archaeological sites receiving state or federal permits, funding, or licenses, and requires developers to hire private archaeology CRM firms to dig before construction. The following year, my wife of one month and I moved to Florida for a year, where I found out the hard way how difficult it was to find archaeology jobs during a recession. We were able to find archaeology work, eventually, where we were able to excavate and rebury several sets of human remains, although it was in the Everglades and we were surrounded by fire ants, lightning, snakes, and alligators.

We fled to Boston in 2008. Again, finding work in archaeology was nearly impossible, so I became a self-employed artist (that is a whole different book) but continued to do independent archaeological study on various collections I had access to around Boston. I also continued a multiyear trend of not getting into graduate school. I did, however, eventually find employment with Public Archaeology Laboratory (PAL), a private nonprofit CRM firm, and had several truly incredible seasons with their amazing crew excavating and romping over sites and miles of power-line corridors throughout New England. In September 2010, I found out that Ellen Berkland, the Boston's city archaeologist at that time, was leaving her position to become the archaeologist for the Department of Conservation and Recreation (DCR). While I was planning on applying to the University of Massachusetts–Boston for its master's program in historical archaeology, the application was not even due for months, and I knew I needed to be at least enrolled in a master's program to be qualified for the job.

Unfortunately for the City Archaeology Program, but fortunately for me, the recession led to a job-hiring freeze for the city, and the position remained vacant for more than one year. During that time, I got into the UMass Boston's master's program in historical archaeology, and I started doing public talks and writing as though I were the city archaeologist. I figured the job would open at some point, and if I could show I had been doing much of the stuff I would be doing as city archaeologist on my own time, it would give me an advantage. It did.

In November 2011, the position finally opened, and within a few weeks I was chosen. That was and will be one of the most surreal and happiest moments of my life. I have since had the honor and pleasure of being the city archaeologist of Boston, where I manage more than one million artifacts excavated from dozens of sites throughout the city, conduct digs on smaller projects on city-owned land, and provide public outreach and education events throughout the year.

I was extremely fortunate in 2013 to receive permission from my superiors in the city to pursue publication of this book and to write it as part of my work, so long as all of the author proceeds go toward the City Archaeology

Program. Because the program relies exclusively on donated labor, funds, and supplies for its work, this book is a major part of our future funding plans for the City Archaeology Program. I want to take this opportunity to thank you for the support you have shown by reading this book, and I hope you enjoy reading it as much as I enjoyed writing it.

Acknowledgments

There are so many people who are directly responsible for the existence of this book. To start, I need to acknowledge all the known and unknown individuals who made, used, and left behind these artifacts, without whom this book would not exist. Thank you to the many groups, individuals, and institutions that assisted in the production of this book by providing free access to images, artifacts, and research, including the Boston Public Library, Boston City Archives, the Massachusetts Historical Commission, Boston University, UMass Boston, Deborah Cox, Jade Luiz, Dennis Piechota, Jennifer Poulsen, Miles Shugar, Elizabeth Solomon, and Gill Solomon. My eternal gratitude and appreciation go to the volunteers of the City Archaeology Program, both in the lab and field, who make this program a success and were directly responsible for finding some of the artifacts featured in this book. I am also grateful to all of the firms, archaeologists, and researchers who have worked in Boston during the past forty-plus years to produce the research, collections, and analysis presented here. Thank you to my mentors, Curtis, Mary, Ellen, and Steve, for showing me the way. My greatest appreciation to my predecessor city archaeologists: Ellen Berkland, Steven Pendery, and Stephen Mrozowski for their work and accomplishments—I truly stand on the shoulders of giants. Thank you to Richard Pult and the University Press of New England for making this so easy. My gratitude to Ellen Lipsey and Nancy Girard, who not only allowed this book to be made as part of my city archaeologist duties, but were its greatest champions. Finally, thank you to my wife, Jen, and my entire family for your collective and unwavering support.

A HISTORY OF BOSTON

IN 50 ARTIFACTS

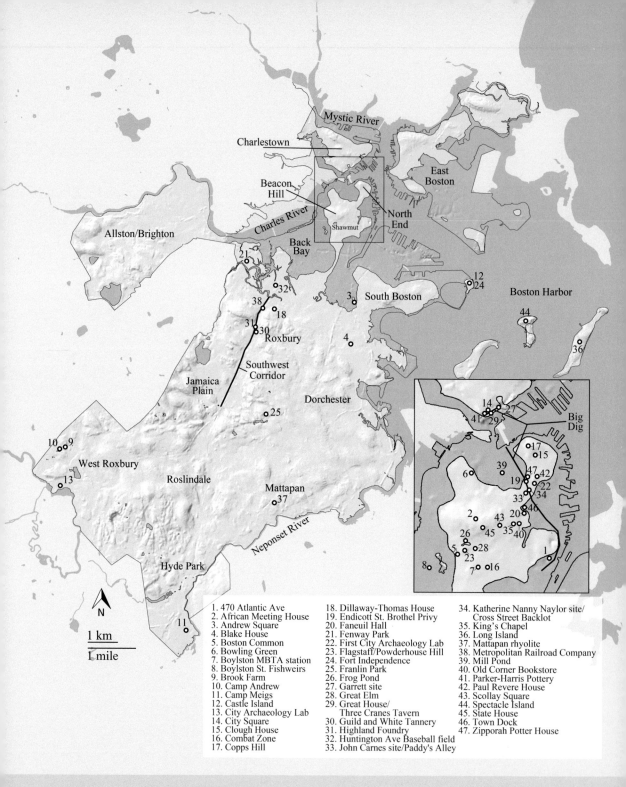

Places and sites mentioned in the text. Map by the author, 2015;
original shoreline (Seasholes 2003).

Legend		
1. 470 Atlantic Ave	18. Dillaway-Thomas House	34. Katherine Nanny Naylor site/
2. African Meeting House	19. Endicott St. Brothel Privy	Cross Street Backlot
3. Andrew Square	20. Faneuil Hall	35. King's Chapel
4. Blake House	21. Fenway Park	36. Long Island
5. Boston Common	22. First City Archaeology Lab	37. Mattapan rhyolite
6. Bowling Green	23. Flagstaff/Powderhouse Hill	38. Metropolitan Railroad Company
7. Boylston MBTA station	24. Fort Independence	39. Mill Pond
8. Boylston St. Fishweirs	25. Franlin Park	40. Old Corner Bookstore
9. Brook Farm	26. Frog Pond	41. Parker-Harris Pottery
10. Camp Andrew	27. Garrett site	42. Paul Revere House
11. Camp Meigs	28. Great Elm	43. Scollay Square
12. Castle Island	29. Great House/	44. Spectacle Island
13. City Archaeology Lab	Three Cranes Tavern	45. State House
14. City Square	30. Guild and White Tannery	46. Town Dock
15. Clough House	31. Highland Foundry	47. Zipporah Potter House
16. Combat Zone	32. Huntington Ave Baseball field	
17. Copps Hill	33. John Carnes site/Paddy's Alley	

Introduction

While Boston's history began many thousands of years ago, the archaeological investigations into this past are a relatively recent development. Decades of professional and avocational archaeological work throughout the area have revealed a complex and personal narrative of Boston's deep history that is only known through archaeological investigation.

The earliest archaeological digs were executed by the Harvard archaeologists Jeffries Wyman (figure 1.1) and Frederic W. Putnam at the shores of New England, where Native sites were highly visible in the form of eroding clam-shell middens.[1] These piled food remains and tool debris left layered deposits that allowed these early anthropologists to begin creating a sequence of stone tool types and forms (see artifact 5 for an example of an artifact from a Boston shell midden).

Charles Willoughby, an artist by trade, met Putnam in Maine during an archaeological survey and developed a passion for local Native material culture. Putnam convinced Willoughby to join the Peabody Museum staff in 1894, where he would eventually become director from 1915 to 1928. His collecting and salvage archaeological excavations in the Boston area in the 1930s further established Harvard's local archaeological interests and grew its archaeological collections in the region.[2]

Arising from the work of these predecessors, avocational archaeologists increased the interest in Massachusetts Native archaeology, resulting in the formation of the Massachusetts Archaeological Society in 1939. In the 1940s, construction in the Back Bay neighborhood of Boston uncovered of portions of the 5,000-year-old Boylston Street fishweirs (artifact 3). This fence-like structure was first encountered in 1914 during construction of the MBTA Green Line down Boylston Street. Frederick Johnson, curator of the R. S. Peabody Museum in Andover, conducted one of the first multidisciplinary surveys of an archaeological site in the country, including pollen, wood, shellfish, sediment, chemistry, and diatom experts, that exceeded the analysis standards of many archaeological digs conducted today.[3]

The work of avocational archaeologists and collectors continued throughout the 1940s, '50s, and '60s. Around the country, the drastic effects of urban-renewal projects, such as the demolition of the West End neighborhood of Boston, spurred the historic preservation movement. In 1966, the National Historic Preservation Act created legislation that, among other things, re-quired that all federally sponsored, funded, and permitted projects be reviewed for their impacts to archaeological sites. This law also created the position of state archaeologist to review federal projects. In Massachusetts, specifically, an additional state law, 950 CMR 71.00, mimics the federal laws expanding the state archaeologist's review to include all *state*-sponsored, -funded, and -permitted projects.

These laws created the need for wider surveys of the region to produce back-ground information that archaeologists could use to make informed decisions on potential archaeological impacts. In the late 1960s, the Harvard-trained archaeologist Dena Dincauze conducted a broad survey of the Charles River Basin, documenting known archaeological sites found through professional and avocational digs as well as contributing newly discovered Native sites. Dincauze created a predictive model for where Native habitation sites could exist in and around Boston, which is still in use today. Another leading woman in archaeology, Barbara Luedtke, began researching Native sites on the Boston Harbor Islands, creating in 1975 an exhaustive survey of the known Native sites in the island network.[4]

Upon the foundations laid by Dincauze, Luedtke, and others on Native archaeological sites, historical archaeologists such as Stanley South, James Deetz, and Ivor Noel Hume, who were working on major seventeenth-cen-tury sites in Massachusetts and Virginia, began demonstrating the value of archaeology on more recent sites. Some of the earliest professional archae-ological surveys conducted in Boston were led by Beth Anne Bower, staff archaeologist for the Museum of African American History. These surveys focused on the African Meeting Houses of Boston and Nantucket as well as historic sites in the historic core of the Roxbury neighborhood of Boston.[5]

In the late 1970s, the growth of Boston had put such stress on the transpor-tation infrastructure that drastic alternatives were needed. This period saw the birth of two transportation projects that would forever change archaeology in Boston and the appearance of the city as a whole.

The Southwest Corridor was a proposed eight-lane highway that would have followed an existing railway line through the neighborhoods of Roxbury, Jamaica Plain, and Hyde Park before continuing south to the town of Canton. The project was controversial because of the proposed eminent-domain removal of mostly lower-income minority housing along the corridor. Although the project never came to fruition (it was later used for the Orange Line MBTA tunnel and a park above), extensive archaeological surveys were conducted all along the route during the planning stages of the project.[6]

These archaeological surveys documented twenty-six historic sites and two Native sites that existed along the former path of the Muddy River.[7] The historic sites documented the early colonial history of Roxbury and later industrial complexes related to ironworking, beer production, and other industries. In total, 447 standard banker's boxes of artifacts were recovered and more than 1,000 pages of archaeological reports were published detailing the complex and diverse history of Boston's Roxbury neighborhood.

THE BIG DIG

The Central Artery/Tunnel project or, as it is more commonly called, the Big Dig, began in the late 1970s. This roughly five-mile-long corridor essentially replaced an existing raised "highway on stilts" with a tunnel. Archaeological surveys in the early 1980s resulted in the identification of dozens of historic and Native sites requiring an extensive archaeological excavation, known as a data recovery. These sites stretched the entire route of the tunnel through Charlestown, downtown, and portions of South Boston. Even Spectacle Island received a large archaeological survey because it was to be the location where the excavated dirt would be piled.[8]

These surveys produced over 2,000 boxes of artifacts (including artifacts 5–6, 9–21, 23–28, 30–31, and 34) and more than 7,000 pages of archaeological reports detailing a great portion of the archaeological knowledge of the city of Boston. The collections are so extensive that they could not be contained in just one repository; they are currently split evenly between the state's archaeological collections facility and a city-owned laboratory space in the North End that would become the City Archaeology Laboratory.

The Big Dig archaeological surveys were producing samples, artifacts, and paperwork at an alarming rate. The basement of a city-owned Tunnel Administration building at 152 North Street in the North End was transformed into a makeshift archaeology lab to process the collections that were coming out of the ground. The state archaeologist urged the City of Boston to hire a city archaeologist who could manage the collections, serve as the public face of archaeology for these projects, and continue to support the city's archaeological needs long after the end of the Big Dig project.[9]

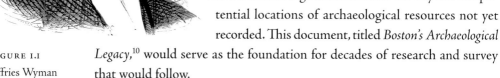

In 1983, the city hired its first city archaeologist, Stephen Mrozowski, using grant money, and created the City Archaeology Program within the Environment Department's Boston Landmarks Commission. Stephen's primary task was to create a formal document that addressed the known archaeological resources in the city and the potential locations of archaeological resources not yet recorded. This document, titled *Boston's Archaeological Legacy*,[10] would serve as the foundation for decades of research and survey that would follow.

FIGURE 1.1
Jeffries Wyman
(Wilder 1875).

In 1985, Stephen Mrozowski left the position of city archaeologist to join the National Park Service's archaeological team in Lowell, Massachusetts, and he eventually went on to become the founder of and a professor at the Andrew Fiske Memorial Center for Archaeological Research at the University of Massachusetts–Boston. The same year Mrozowski departed, Steven Pendery was hired to replace the "first Steve," and he continued as city archaeologist for the next eight years. During this time, Pendery saw the transformation of the city archaeologist from a contract position funded by state and federal grants into a full-time staff-level employee of the City of Boston. Pendery partnered with the city's Parks and Recreation Department on a number of major archaeological surveys, including Boston Common, Franklin Park, and Brook Farm, discovering many of the artifacts shown in this book (artifacts 2, 4, 7, 29, 32, 33, 35, 37–39, 41, 48, and 50). In 1993, Pendery followed the pattern of the first Steve, leaving the city archaeologist position to become the northeast region's head archaeologist for the National Park Service.

Sadly, the city did not fill the position of city archaeologist for nearly two years. In 1994, at the urging of the Boston Landmarks Commission, the city archaeologist position was taken over by Ellen Berkland, a veteran of the Big Dig archaeological surveys. Because the program had been reduced to a part-time contract position, some progress had been lost. Despite this, Ellen immediately revived the City Archaeology Program's public-outreach efforts focusing on public presentations and school visits to the City Archaeology Lab, which was still located in the basement of 152 North Street. Ellen would lead the program for the next fifteen years, growing its national reputation, supervising hundreds of archaeology students (many of whom went on to receive BAS, MAS, and PhDs in archaeology, myself included), and instructing thousands of Boston schoolchildren in Boston's archaeological heritage. Ellen left the position in 2010 to become the senior archaeologist for the Massachusetts Department of Conservation and Recreation (DCR).

As a result of budget issues during the slow recovery following the Great Recession, a hiring freeze prevented the city archaeologist position from being filled. In 2011, the city decided to sell the 152 North Street property, which was nearly empty except for a mothballed City Archaeology Laboratory in its basement filled with nearly 2,000 boxes of the city's history. Realizing the challenge of properly moving these collections, the then director of the Boston Landmarks Commission, Ellen Lipsey, was finally able to use the sale of the building to convince the city to open the position of city archaeologist.

After weeks of interviews, I received a phone call in November 2011 offering me the position of city archaeologist. My first tasks were to pack the lab for the move and to work with the city's property managers to prepare the new lab location. Four months later, the entire contents of the City Archaeology Lab moved to a renovated doctor's office and credit union inside the former headquarters of the National Grid utility company at 201 Rivermoor Street in West Roxbury. The nearly 4,000-square-foot facility is a massive improvement over the previous lab, and allows the staff to manage the collections with enough space for anticipated growth of the collections in the future.

Once the lab moved, the City Archaeology Program reopened in earnest and has since received thousands of hours of artifact processing from more than one hundred volunteers. Although the city archaeologist is a full-time staff position, at the time of the publication of this book it is the only paid staff position and the only funding the City Archaeology Program receives. It is through the dedication of dozens of active volunteers that our digs, lab work, and public events succeed. The program's Facebook and Twitter accounts have become the public face of the City Archaeology Program and feature our work and efforts to make Boston's archaeology visible. With nearly 400 documented archaeological sites spanning thousands of years of human history, I believe that Boston has one of the most—if not *the* most—interesting and one of the broadest assemblages of archaeological sites of any major US city.

I write this book out of a genuine love of Boston archaeology and the stories it reveals. I hope that these stories bring a new perspective into and appreciation for the lives of the people that live and lived in Boston—one that goes beyond many of the well-worn tales of major historic figures and events. It is also my hope that this book will bring new attention to the archaeology of Boston and the need for a robust and well-funded City Archaeology Program. To this end, every last nickel of the proceeds from the sale of this book will go toward funding the City Archaeology Program and supporting the digs, lab work, and public outreach that makes the program an important public resource.

This book is divided into five parts. Each of these parts represents a discrete period of history, but they are not equal in timespan. Part 1 contains artifacts from the Massachusett Native people that have been living in Shawmut, the place we now call Boston, for thousands of years. Part 2 covers the early colonial and Puritan history of the city, from its founding in 1630 to 1700, as Boston developed in the early history of America. Part 3 explores the industries and individuals that transformed Boston from just another town into a city with its own identity in the lead-up to war between 1700 and 1775. Part 4 includes artifacts that can be directly tied to the Revolutionary War era, a brief but pivotal moment in history that shaped the city and the country as a whole. Finally, part 5 covers postrevolutionary Boston, as its population grew and new groups of people began to immigrate to the city, helping to create the diverse and vibrant communities seen today. It is my hope that this book will ignite an interest in the physical and personal stories of Boston's past through the stuff that has been left behind.

Boston did not begin in 1630. Boston's history does not begin with Governor Winthrop. It does not even begin with William Blaxton, its first European settler. History is the story of the human past. Thousands, if not millions, of people lived in the place we now call Boston well before the first European arrived. It was 12,000 years ago, soon after the glacier retreated, that Native Americans began exploring and settling the land that was a very different Boston. While we have yet to find the telltale artifact from this earliest time, the fluted point, in what was Boston, the presence of such stone tools in the surrounding towns, including Saugus, Canton, and Watertown, show that people were living in and around Boston.

Archaeologists have been studying the Native history of Massachusetts for decades. Their research has resulted in the division of Native history into three broad time periods: the Paleoindian, Archaic, and Woodland periods. These divisions in time mark what scientists see as significant changes in cultural practices and artifact types. In general, the Paleoindian period represents the time between 12,000 and 10,000 BP (years "before present"), during which some of the earliest

people to settle in Massachusetts arrived. They survived mainly on coastal resources such as birds and fish, coupled with megafauna that included woolly mammoth and caribou.[1] The environment of Boston would have looked more like the northern Alaska tundra. The Archaic period (10,000–3000 BP) saw the greater use of seasonal camps, carved stone bowls, and settlements along rivers and the coast. By the Woodland period (3000–400 BP), pottery, the bow and arrow, and agriculture had been developed. The stabilizing of climate and sea levels during the Woodland period allowed for villages to develop, as food became more reliable and predictable and populations grew. These villages were centered at the mouths of rivers and in coastal regions like the Boston area.

If Boston's 12,000-year human history time line were one hundred inches long, the last three inches would be the time after 1630. That means 97 percent of Boston's history, its human story, occurs prior to the arrival of Europeans, so naturally this book will start with the real beginning of the story—the arrival of Native Americans in the area.

I. Mattapan Banded Rhyolite

600,000,000 BP | Mattapan

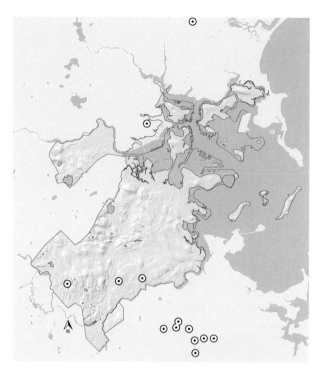

If you were to map the location of places in New England where one could find the right type of stone to make stone tools, one thing that would become immediately clear is how many of them are located in and around Boston (figure 1.1), including Mattapan banded rhyolite, the stone featured as our first artifact. This stone, along with many others used by Native people in Boston, formed around six hundred million years ago in a series of volcanic eruptions that formed the Blue Hills, the hills of Lynn, and many smaller hills in between. Besides the raw stone tool resources, its low-lying basin surrounded by mountains with easy

FIGURE 1.1
Map of Boston with sources of stone suitable for use in stone tool production shown by dots. Map by the author.

access to numerous river systems and the ocean made Boston a major draw for the first people to arrive in the area around 12,000 years ago, the people that archaeologists call the Paleoindians.

During the Paleoindian period, sea levels were many dozens of feet lower than they are today, which meant that one would be able to walk from what would one day become downtown Boston, due east, for nearly ten miles without getting one's feet wet. These first people would have been following the megafauna (mammoth, caribou, mastodon, and so on) that would have roamed the tundra-like landscape left behind by the retreating Laurentian glacier, while also utilizing the bird and fish resources abundant in the surrounding rivers and ocean.

Paleoindians can be most easily recognized in the archaeological record by their distinctive stone spear points, called fluted points, similar to the one shown in figure 1.2. Although fluted points have been found in Saugus, Wakefield, Canton,[1] and other nearby areas, there has never been a fluted point discovered in Boston, leaving open the possibility that archaeologists may still be able to extend the history of Boston at least another 2,000 years if one of these is ever found archaeologically.

The oldest datable site in Boston was found on Long Island in 1984; it was about 8,000 to 10,000 years old. During this period, Boston's climate warmed as the glacier continued to retreat, and the landscape transformed from a tundra-like region of low scrub and small evergreens to a forested environment with well-established river systems, including the Charles, Mystic, and Neponset. The 1984 dig was part of an archaeological survey of Long Island and Deer Island testing areas for a proposed wastewater treatment plant.[2] Because of the importance of the intact Native archaeological resources on Long Island, archaeologists determined that massive archaeological excavations would be needed if the wastewater treatment plant were located there. The planners chose the alternative location on Deer Island for the massive treatment plant and its iconic "egg" digestive tanks.

During this early period, well before the harbor formed, the Neponset River flowed past the UMass Boston campus and South Boston, converging with the Charles River near Castle Island before flowing east to the sea. This "paleo–Charles River" and the now-extinct river that once flowed north from Weymouth created two parallel river systems that flowed on either side of what would become Spectacle, Long, Gallop's, George's, and Lovell's Islands. Native people would have found the area that would become Boston Harbor an ideal location to live, for it provided easy access to river and ocean wildlife, while also being accessible to multiple river systems for quick transport to seasonal inland camps. The Long Island site likely served as one of these seasonal base camps because it was located in close proximity to the two rivers.

FIGURE 1.2
Fluted point made from Pennsylvania jasper found in Chatham, Massachusetts.

2. Neville Point

7500–5500 BP | Boston Common

By far the most undeveloped area in all of downtown Boston is the Common, and because of this lack of development, it has been on our archaeological radar for decades. The broken spear point shown as our second artifact was found near the Frog Pond during the 1986 archaeological survey of Boston Common conducted by my predecessor, Steven Pendery (Boston's second city archaeologist), and a team of volunteers.[1] Each of the light poles and electrical junction boxes existing on the Common today required the excavation of an archaeological test pit, which documented what was preserved in the ground prior to the construction. These types of digs conducted before development, generally referred to as cultural resource management (CRM), are common in Boston and throughout the United States.

We can tell by the overall shape of a stone tool roughly when it was made, because Native tool shapes often remained consistent for hundreds to thousands of years before changing. This tool's tree-like triangular shape and a distinct stem or trunk indicates that it was made between 5,500 and 7,500 years ago, during a period in Boston's history that archaeologists call the Middle Archaic. During this period, we see a distinct increase in the number of sites in Boston, including downtown, Roxbury, West Roxbury, Jamaica Plain,

FIGURE 2.1
View of empty Frog Pond toward the State House with the Frog Pond site in the foreground.

FIGURE 2.2

Circa 1750 view
south from Mt.
Vernon toward
Boston Common
showing the former
shoreline and
Fox Hill (Byron
ca. 1750; image
courtesy of the
Boston Public
Library).

and Boston Harbor, indicating that Native populations and site creations were growing at the time.

When this point was made, the Charles River would have flowed only a few hundred feet west of where the point was found, near the Frog Pond on the Common (figure 2.1). From this location, the people who were camping or hunting in the area would have been able to hike to the top of Beacon Hill to observe animals or other Native people in the area, and they could also have easy access to the Charles River for transportation throughout the region.

This tool is likely a knife or spear point, because it was made many thousands of years before the bow and arrow was used in Massachusetts. Similar points found near Carver were excavated with stone weights used to balance an atlatl.[2] Atlatls are spear-throwing devices that can be found all over the world. They work much like the handheld tennis-ball thrower used today for dogs—by extending the length of the arm, they allowed increased thrust to be applied behind the atlatl's dart (which is similar in appearance to a hand-thrown spear). It is probable that this Neville point served as the tip of a dart.

The stone material that this point is made from is Blue Hills rhyolite, a type of stone found only in the hills south of Boston in Quincy and Milton. Over time, its original dark-blue/gray color has weathered in the acidic soil of Boston to a whitish chalky color. This stone formed 600 million years ago out of cooled lava from a massive volcano that once existed at the southern end of Boston.[3]

The spear point is missing its tip. Typically, hunters would retrieve their spears and other hunting tools after the hunt. Bringing them back to their base camp, they would have resharpened their spear tips or made new ones to replace those that were lost. The Frog Pond site would have been located just east of the former Boston shoreline (figure 2.2), making the camp ideal for hunting, stone tool work, and transportation. Because we recovered only the base of this point, we can speculate that the hunter thought it was too broken to resharpen the point, was in a rush and discarded it, or had enough raw materials or replacement points that he didn't need to worry about the loss of one point base.

Boston Common is a place visited by millions of Bostonians and visitors each year, but the same hills and open spaces that are loved today were equally appreciated by the Native Americans who lived in the exact same landscape for many thousands of years.

3. Fishweir Stakes

5300–3700 BP | Back Bay

The Boylston Street fishweirs were first discovered in 1913 during the excavation of massive trenches along Boylston Street for the first streetcar system in Boston.[1] An estimated 65,000 sharpened, twisted, and crushed stakes and sticks were found in gray marine clay embedded what used to be Boston's Back Bay. The area that is currently the South End and Back Bay neighborhoods used to be a large tidal mudflat before it was filled in the mid-1800s. Twice a day, tides would move up the Charles River and flood the muddy flats to create a large brackish bay.

The stakes and sticks encountered in 1913 were immediately identified as a wooden fishweir similar to ones still in use by fishermen in Canada and other areas at the time. Weirs are fence-like structures made out of sticks, rocks, or other materials and placed within a waterway to channel or trap moving fish (figure 3.1). Each spring, millions of anadromous fish, including herring and alewife (figure 3.2) would swim upriver, spawn, and return to the sea. While less common today than in the past, weirs are still in use around the world for passive fish harvesting. Five construction projects in the Back Bay have documented encountering fishweirs there since 1913.

Because the weir stakes are wood, we have been able to use carbon-14 dating to determine the age of the structure. The results of multiple samples show that the Boylston Street and other Back Bay fishweirs were made and in use over an incredibly long period between 3,600 and 5,200 years ago. This is the same time period during which Neolithic peoples were building Stonehenge and Egyptians were building the pyramids of Giza. Careful excavations and documentation of preserved weir deposits in the 1980s revealed that instead of comprising one vast fence structure, the weirs were built and rebuilt in small

FIGURE 3.1
View of a reconstructed fishweir built by the Fishweir Project each May.

FIGURE 3.2
Alewife (*Alosa
pseudoharengus*)
(Edmonson and
Chrisp 1927–1940).

segments over the entire 2,000 years Native people used this technology in the Back Bay.[2] The shape and location of the weirs indicated that they were used to channel spawning fish from the center of the bay toward the former shoreline, where Native people could scoop up or spear them by the hundreds or thousands. Although they have not yet been found, there likely would have been nearby drying stations where the fish could be preserved through smoking, allowing them to be used as a stable food source for months.

The stakes in the jar shown in the main photo were encountered in 1946 during construction of the Berkeley Building (Old Hancock Building). A lawyer was walking along the Back Bay and noticed the sticks pictured here and others coming out of the construction lot. Realizing from the major report on the weirs published a few years earlier that they were part of the Boylston Street fishweirs, he collected the sticks, put them in a jar, filled the jar with water, and placed it on his mantle. Nearly seventy years later, the lawyer, then on his deathbed, told his daughter that someone who knew about the weirs needed to have the jar. His daughter took the sticks to Ellen Berkland (Boston's third city archaeologist) at the City Archaeology Lab and donated the still-unopened jar to the City of Boston. These weir stakes remain some of the only aboveground weir fragments, though thousands, perhaps millions, still reside forty feet beneath the streets of Back Bay.

Like many of those encountered during construction over the past one hundred years, the weir stakes in the photo exhibit a bent or zigzag shape. This is because the weir has been buried under thirty to forty feet of clay and fill for thousands of years, which has slowly crushed and compressed the weir stakes into their crooked shape. Around 2,600 years ago, the Back Bay fishweirs were abandoned. It is likely that the rising seas coupled with larger and stronger tides made the short and fragile weirs too difficult to maintain. The remaining fishweirs gradually collapsed and were buried in more than fifteen feet of marine clay. In the mid-1800s, Back Bay was filled, depositing an additional fifteen feet of dirt and debris on top of which the Back Bay neighborhood was built.

The preservation of organic materials such as these sticks is exceedingly rare in Boston's acidic soils. The continued existence of the Back Bay fishweirs beneath the bustling streets and buildings of the Back Bay is a lasting reminder of the presence of Native Americans in Boston's past and their continued presence today.

4. Native Pottery

1600–1000 BP | Boston Common, Downtown

Organic artifacts are rare in New England, and when preserved archaeologically they are of great importance (artifacts 6, 13, 14, 16, 17, 19, 42, 44, and 45). The pine and evergreen trees found throughout the area have dropped acidic needles in the soils for thousands of years,

FIGURE 4.1 Early conical Native pottery form circa 3000–2000 BP (*left*) with later incised collared and globular form circa 1000–400 BP (*right*) (Fowler 1966, 52 and 60; used with permission by the Massachusetts Archaeological Society).

producing ground unfriendly to the preservation of delicate plant and animal remains. Because of this preservation issue, we lack entire swaths of material culture—including fabric—that undoubtedly played critical roles in daily life.

The two typical ways fabric can "preserve" belowground in New England is through carbonation (burning) or through a cast. The artifact in the main photo is an example of fabric's "echo" preserved as a cast in clay. This fragment of Native ceramic was found at the Frog Pond site on Boston Common and was made from thick coils of local glacial clay, easily accessible in nearby river streams. While forming clay into the cone-shaped vessel typical of this period, the Native craftsperson used a pad or cloth made from woven threads to support the vessel, to provide decoration, or to employ as a paddling device to combine the coils in the vessel. The wet clay recorded the impression of this fabric, and when the potter fired the vessel, the impression became permanent.

Native pottery technology began in Boston around 3,000 years ago. The earliest vessels were lightly fabric-paddled on their interior and exterior walls. Over time, various distinct decorations were developed that today help archaeologists determine the age of a ceramic type. These vessels were fired in open-fire pits, which made a usable cooking or storage pot, but they were fragile, resulting in breakage during use, as well as through frost expansion while pots lay buried in the ground. Because of this fragility, to date this is the largest piece of Native pottery excavated in Boston. The fragmentary state of pottery in New England means that in order to determine the overall size and form of local pottery, archaeologists have to rely heavily on the rare instances where most of a Native vessel remained in place in the ground, ready to be reconstructed.

In Boston and the surrounding region, Native pottery was most commonly conical in shape (figure 4.1). This shape seems impractical today but is found throughout history and around the world, because the cone base is stronger than a curved base, and it also allows the vessel to sit easily in soft ground or be wedged into a cooking fire. About 1,000 years ago, a new style of pottery came to New England from New York. This type had a round base, constricted neck, and flared or crown-like rims. Usually the crown rims had linear incised lines drawn into them, similar to the fragment of pottery shown in figure 4.2, also found on Boston Common. These pots were similar in function to the earlier types, but the narrow neck allowed Native people to tie a cord around the vessel and suspend it over a fire, rather than set it directly in the hearth.

Based on comparable examples of pottery of this thickness and decoration, it is likely that the original pot was made between 1,000 and 2,000 years ago, during a period of Boston's history archaeologists call the Middle Woodland. The archaeological record during this period is particularly fascinating because it appears that trade routes throughout New England flourished, resulting in people and goods traveling great distances. It is not uncommon on sites of this period to find stone tools made from raw stone materials that are only found naturally in Pennsylvania, Maine, and New York, indicating that these goods were being picked up, carried, and traded across great distances. Even more interesting is that around 1,000 years ago, this wide-ranging trade seems to vanish, and tools suddenly are being made from the most local materials available. We still are trying to figure out what happened.

FIGURE 4.2
Incised Native pottery from Boston Common.

This pottery fragment was found just a few feet from the much older Neville point (artifact 2), meaning that several periods of Native habitation spanning thousands of years existed at the same location.[1] The site itself is located on the southern slope of Beacon Hill. Prior to the cementing of the pond for the wading pool and skating rink so loved today, the Frog Pond was a freshwater natural spring that flowed from the base of Beacon Hill and then westward into Back Bay and the Charles River, which at the time would have been located only about 1,000 feet away. Here people would have had the protection of the hill, which also served as a high point to view the entire area, fresh water, the Charles River, the nearby harbor, and all the resources available in these locations. It is no wonder there is evidence of occupation for thousands of years.

5. Fish Spear

2000–1500 BP | Spectacle Island, Boston Harbor

Because a great deal of time and energy was devoted to finding and processing food, especially in the deep past, the vast majority of the artifacts we encounter on Native archaeological sites directly relate to food. Shell middens were some of the first Native American cultural sites to be explored by archaeologists (figure 5.1). The middens' distinct black soils filled with thousands of white shells stand out strongly in coastal deposits along the shores of the region's bays and islands, and they attracted early archaeologists as far back as the 1860s. Middens are large deposits of refuse, typically dark in color because of the large amounts of organic food remains. This color and greasy texture can last thousands of years after they are first deposited. Shell middens are particularly important to archaeologists because the calcium carbonate in the shells lowers the acidity of the normally acidic New England soils to a point at which bone can be preserved. This preservation makes these middens the *only* place to find ancient Native bone artifacts on an archaeological site.

Bone tools would have been commonplace in the past, but archaeologists do not often have the luxury of including them in their analyses because of these preservation issues. These barbed bone spears from a 1,000 year-old shell midden deposit at Spectacle Island would have been used for fishing in Boston Harbor or many nearby rivers, and were probably very prominent artifacts in the daily tool kit of any Native person. The artifact in the main photo, a fish spear, was found on Spectacle Island in Boston Harbor (figure 5.2) during archaeological investigations as part of the Big Dig and represents just one of the many tool types used to acquire food from the land and sea.[1]

Bone spears were probably carved using some sort of stone tool. Formal tools were probably not necessary to work the bone in these points, so roughly broken pieces of rhyolite or other local stone tool material were likely used to generally shape the spears. Once shaped, their points were sharpened by grinding them on one of the many available abrasive stones or a wet-sand-covered rock. The bone itself is likely part of a deer long bone. Leg bones

FIGURE 5.1
Broken clamshells from a Native shell midden in Frog Pond on Boston Common.

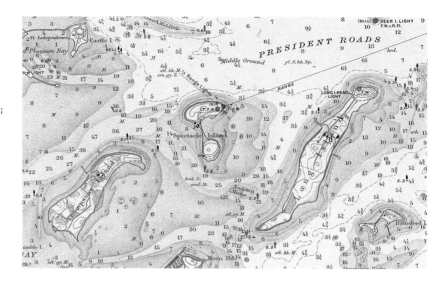

could be broken with a large rock to extract nutritious marrow. Shattered long bones of deer are common occurrences at shell middens. The bone itself would have been used for tools and the marrow eaten for its high nutrient content.

Sometimes artifacts can imply the existence of other artifacts, technology, or actions that do not survive. For example, you could assume that if you found a bobbin on an archaeological site, there was probably a needle, thread, some sort of fabric, and the act of sewing going on at a site. Similarly, although these bone spears could be used from the shoreline, they were more likely part of a canoe fishing kit, implying the presence of a boat and a spear that would have held the bone tip.

Canoes would have been made from large trees. Axes were made by polishing stones into sharpened blades, an extremely time-consuming process; to make the wood softer so that the axe-work was not as hard, fires would be set around the base of a tree. Once the tree was felled, it would be hollowed out. This fire also burned away and weakened portions of the interior wood, and adze blades were used to remove large portions of the wood by hand. The net result of this work was a canoe-shaped vessel consisting of a single tree trunk, with room for several individuals inside and capable of traversing lakes, rivers, and the ocean. These types of vessels, called *mishoon* in the local Massachusett language, have been found at the bottom of several natural ponds throughout Massachusetts and are still made by local tribal groups today.

Creations like this bone spear were made for specific purposes—in this case fish spearing—yet their physical properties, their raw materials, and their actual use can give us much more information about the history and life of the Native peoples that call Boston home.

6. Massachusett Weaving

In the early 1990s, construction workers were excavating soils in the vicinity of 470 Atlantic Avenue in Boston's financial district. At approximately thirty feet belowground, they came across a crumpled organic mass inside a deep deposit of marine clay. The crumpled mass was transported from the construction site to the City Archaeology Lab in Boston's North End, where it was placed in a box in the collections storage area of the lab. Twenty years later, a volunteer researcher at the lab found it in a shelved box and brought it to my attention. On the basis of the depth at which the discovery was made, which was conveniently written on the bag it was stored in, and the fact that the material used in it was some sort of woven grass or reed, it was possible that it represented an early Native creation.

In order to confirm whether it was in fact old, a small sample of the material was sent to a lab to date the material using carbon-14 accelerated mass spectrometer (AMS) dating techniques. The results of this test revealed that it dated to between AD 1454 and 1565, which makes this the largest and oldest piece of preserved woven material ever found in the Northeast.

During conservation at UMass Boston's Fiske Center for Archaeological Research, the sample was gently opened, thus revealing that it consists of two segments of parallel woven strips interwoven to create a slightly triangular-shaped fragment. The two strips were created by weaving reed-like material in a twill pattern, where one warp element passes over two weft elements (instead of a one-over-one standard basket weave) (figure 6.1). A cord was also found that consists of a twisted element of reed doubled onto itself (figure 6.2). This cord was incorporated into the edge of the weaving to reinforce the edge of the material. On the basis of its size and shape, as well as comparative examples at the Peabody Museum of Archaeology at Harvard, it appears that this is an element of a larger basket or mat made by a Native person and lost off the shore of Boston nearly 500 years ago.

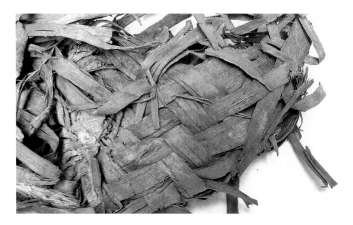

FIGURE 6.1
Detail of plaited weave of fibers.

FIGURE 6.2
Detail of woven
fragments and
spun fibers.

The area around 470 Atlantic Avenue, almost adjacent to the former dock where tea was thrown into the harbor in protest on December 17, 1773, used to be open water and tidal mudflats before colonial land making filled the area. In the fifteenth century, this area would have been just offshore of what would later be named Fort Hill. The hill was removed in 1869, but before the arrival of Europeans it would have been an excellent lookout point facing the shallow bay (later to be named Fort Point Channel) and the northern mudflats surrounding what would become South Boston. This area would have been easy walking distance to both the western portion of the original Shawmut peninsula, passing the Frog Pond site mentioned previously to reach the Charles River, and to the east to the resources of the mudflats (clams) and the entire Boston Harbor area.

Perhaps the individual who made or used this weaving was collecting clams in the mudflats or harvesting fish from a fishweir in the tidal area. Perhaps it was a mat used in or on a *wetu*, a domed house made from bent wooden limbs and covered in bark sheets or woven mats, that blew away in the strong winds of the area. No matter what its original use, it landed in the water or mud (depending on the tide) just offshore and became embedded in the clayey deposit, where it was slowly buried by natural sediments before being ultimately capped by fill in the ever-growing city that appeared above it.

The Massachusett-Ponkapoag people, whose ancestral land included Shawmut, the place we now call Boston, created this and the other artifacts discussed previously. Although disease, land loss, and the acts of colonial oppression reduced the population of the local Massachusett tribe, their presence in the Boston community continues to this day.

7. Arrowhead

Circa 1600–1625 | Boston Common, Downtown

The Great Elm was a monumental American elm tree located near the center of Boston Common. First recorded in early eighteenth-century maps in mature form, it was a major feature of the landscape until it fell during a hurricane in 1876. In 1986, archaeologists conducting a dig near the former location of the Great Elm (figure 7.1) found a small triangular piece of copper. It was cataloged as a copper fragment until 2013, when it reemerged during a rebagging and resorting exercise of the Boston Common archaeological assemblage. The small, almost nondescript copper triangle was reidentified as a Native arrowhead. The first European visitors to the region in the late 1500s and early 1600s would have likely encountered Massachusett people on the open ocean because both were actively traveling through and using the abundant resources of the harbor. Copper was a relatively common artifact among Europeans, but to the Massachusett people they encountered who had never seen copper or other metals, this material was of great value.

Copper kettles became one of the most common goods traded with Native people in the early seventeenth century. These artifacts would have been ideal for cooking, but many Native people wanted the kettles not for cooking (clay pots still appeared to be preferred) but for the raw materials they were made from, which could be reworked into other creations including arrowheads, beads, and decorative elements for clothing or jewelry.

The triangular shape of this arrowhead is similar to the triangular-shaped stone arrowheads that would have been in daily use just prior to the arrival of Europeans in Boston. Once it was realized that the copper could be transformed relatively easily into a sharp arrowhead, these copper artifacts quickly

FIGURE 7.1
An 1860 view of the Great Elm in Boston Common (*Boston Common* 1860; image courtesy of the Boston Public Library).

started replacing stone arrowheads that were made around the same time for the same purpose (figure 7.2). This is the first and only copper arrowhead found in Boston.

It is interesting that the arrowhead was found so close to the Great Elm of Boston Common. The Great Elm was located at the eastern base of Flagstaff Hill, the central and prominent hill within the Common. This elm was large enough to feature prominently on the 1722 Bonner map, suggesting that less than one hundred years after the founding of Boston the tree had already grown to a size that justified featuring it on maps. Elms grow relatively slowly, so it is likely that the tree itself would have been present in the landscape well before the arrival of Europeans. This means that Native people would have seen and interacted with the younger Great Elm long before Europeans arrived. William Wood stated in the early 1630s that the young city of Boston lacked trees, thus requiring its first inhabitants to seek wood from nearby towns.[1] It is probable that the pressure to find wood in Shawmut, the place that would become Boston, was so great that by the time Europeans arrived, many of the trees in and around Boston would have already been cut, further emphasizing the size and grandeur of what would be called the Great Elm.

There can be no doubt that the Great Elm played a role in the cultural landscape of the Massachusett. It is likely that the copper point was dropped by a person who traveled to or near the Great Elm for one of the many resources it would have provided: shade, an easy gathering place, and a local landmark; humans also tend to gravitate to large, prominent trees in open spaces because of their size and beauty.

This arrowhead was probably produced sometime in the early 1600s after the first European explorers began to traverse the area, but before 1625, when William Blaxton settled near Boston Common and the local Massachusett people retreated westward ahead of the oncoming European invasion. This single arrowhead represents an overlap of cultures and a transition between two groups of people that would forever change the historical narrative of the place that would become Boston.

FIGURE 7.2
Levanna arrowhead
excavated from
Boston Common.

PART 2 Puritanical Foundations
(1629–1700)

This book refers to "Boston" using its contemporary boundary lines, but in 1630, what we consider to be Boston was in fact all or parts of the independent towns of Charlestown, Dorchester, Roxbury, and Watertown. Over many years, these towns broke into smaller towns, portions of which were later incorporated into the modern city of Boston. Throughout the remainder of the book, I will include artifacts in the category of *Boston* even if they were not actually in Boston when they were deposited.

The European settlement of Boston in the early 1600s began a radical and permanent transformation of the tiny peninsula of Shawmut and the surrounding area from a relatively treeless spit of land into the urban metropolis of today. The Puritans and others who settled Boston sought both freedom to practice their religious beliefs outside the watchful eye of the Church of England and opportunities to pursue economic and personal growth in the newly available land and natural resources.

Between 1625 and 1630, the towns of Charlestown, Dorchester, Roxbury, and Watertown were all settled, each by a similar band of Puritans, forming independent communities that would eventually be absorbed, in their entirety or in part, into the City of Boston. Charlestown's first settlement was centered on a point of land at the mouth of the Charles River (now City Square), Boston's near the open bay facing the harbor (now the Old State House), Watertown's where the Charles River Estuary ends, Roxbury's at the base of Boston Neck near Dudley Square, and Dorchester's near Savin Hill.

This part discusses the early colonial history of Boston, its foundations in Charlestown, and the later rise of the city around Town Cove. Artifacts in this part are concentrated in the earliest seventeenth-century archaeological sites found in Charlestown and the North End and the information they reveal about gender, class, and home life in early Boston.

8. Trade Weight

1485–1547 | Boston Harbor

The first Europeans to make the journey across the Atlantic to arrive in Boston would have encountered a land inhabited by thousands of Native peoples living along Boston's shores and rivers. John Cabot appears to be the first documented European to pass alongside the Massachusetts coast in 1498, although his interactions with Native peoples were likely limited, aside from a possible encounter with Native peoples fishing in the harbor. Few explorers ventured near Massachusetts in the sixteenth century, although later Samuel de Champlain (1604–1606) and John Smith (1614), some of the first Europeans to explore the region, likely interacted with residents of coastal Massachusetts (and may be the possible source of the copper used in artifact 7). The first documented European settler in Boston was William Blaxton.

Blaxton arrived in 1623 on a ship that landed in the future town of Weymouth. While most of the surviving passengers returned in 1625, Blaxton traveled north to the Shawmut peninsula, settling on the westernmost peak of a three-hill ridge (called the Trimount or Tremont) that dominated the Boston landscape. Blaxton would leave by 1630, after the residents of Charlestown moved south across the Charles River.

Sadly, Blaxton's house site was lost when the western hill of the Trimount, the notorious red-light district of Mount Vernon (a.k.a. Mt. Whoredom), was removed to fill in the shores of an expanding Boston around 1805. Overall, these explorers and settlers from the seventeenth century and earlier left relatively little behind. You can imagine that when ships were so infrequent, you would be exceedingly careful both with what you brought with you on the boat and how you handled those objects. When it could be weeks to months before you could get restocked, you were far less likely to bring fragile goods, were very careful with what you did bring, and were much more likely to reuse what you had in every possible way. In addition, there was a heavy reliance on Native foods and technologies, many of which, being organic in nature, do not preserve well (artifact 6 is an exception). The net result is relatively few non-Native artifacts left behind in Boston prior to 1630.

The circular brass disk in the main photo is a rare exception. Found on one of the Boston Harbor Islands in 2014, this disk is relatively unadorned except for the marking of the letter *h* with a crown above it (figure 8.1). Archaeologists specializing in the medieval frequently find these disks in England, where they were used as trade weights[1] by merchants and traders to weigh goods against a standard measurement

FIGURE 8.1
Detail of the
crowned *h*
hallmark.

FIGURE 8.2
Trade weight as it
would have been
used in balance
scales.

(figure 8.2). The hallmark on the disk indicates that it had been approved as having met the king's standard weight. Often these disks would get re-hallmarked as the monarchs changed. This particular hallmark is that of Henry VII and VIII, whose combined reigns date from 1485 to 1547.

Since this weight did not receive "updates" of other monarchs, it likely means that it never made it back to England to be restamped. Does this represent the first and only physical evidence left behind by fifteenth- or sixteenth-century explorers in Boston? Is it a traded object that was carried to the area by Native people from elsewhere? Could this have been a very old object still in circulation or use during the seventeenth century, when far greater numbers of Europeans were moving about Boston? We may never know the true history of the object, but it is one of the oldest non-Native artifacts ever found in the United States.

9. Stone from Great House

1629 | City Square, Charlestown

Boston's earliest European settlement sites and houses are exceedingly difficult to find, archaeologically. Unlike many early seventeenth-century British settlements to the south, early towns in the Northeast colonies have tended to remain centered on their original settlement pattern, resulting in the reuse of original properties, streets, and land lots—sometimes for more than 400 years. Boston is no exception. The original settlement on the Shawmut peninsula, which would later become downtown Boston, was begun by William Blaxton, who lived on the south-facing slope of the three-hill ridge called the Trimount or, in the local parlance, "Tremont," and he gardened in what would become Boston Common.

Our earliest surviving European settlement sites have been found in the Charlestown neighborhood of Boston. In protest of the actions of King Charles I, John Winthrop (figure 9.1) signed an agreement with the Massachusetts Bay Colony in August 1629 to lead a fleet of eleven ships housing 700 men, women, and children to the new colony in Salem.[1] Winthrop arrived in Salem that same year.

In 1629, approximately one hundred individuals moved from Salem to the sparsely settled peninsula north of Shawmut to lay out streets, divide land into two-acre lots, and construct a Great House in the town's center.[2] This town, named Charlestown after King Charles I, was settled by Winthrop and his fleet on July 6, 1630. That summer was not kind to the original settlers, and after many deaths, the townspeople, blaming the illnesses on freshwater tainted by the salty harbor, decided to relocate to Shawmut, where numerous freshwater springs were located and in active use by Blaxton. It is here that Winthrop founded the city of Boston in 1630.

FIGURE 9.1
John Winthrop
(Wilson and Fiske
1889, 571).

For many years, the exact location of Winthrop's 1629 Great House was up for debate. The alignment of streets radiating from the City Square area of Charlestown gave an indication of the original center of town. City Square was the original heart of Charlestown, both physically and culturally. After the burning of Charlestown in 1775, the entire center was left permanently undeveloped. Archaeology conducted in City Square before the Big Dig tunnel was later dug through the area not only revealed the Pompeii-like preservation of the City Square and its centerpiece, the Three Cranes Tavern, but also, coupled with in-depth historical research, provided archaeological evidence that a portion of the tavern had once been the original 1629 Great House[3] (figure 9.2).

The stone shown in the main photo is a piece of ballast flint. It was combined with one of hundreds of glacially worn cobbles that were picked up individually and stacked to form the foundation of the Great House, which began as the modest structure that housed not only Governor Winthrop but the settlement's General Court. It sat beneath the building for its one-year existence before becoming part of the wine cellar of the Three Cranes Tavern. For many decades it lay underground, until the fires of the Battle of Bunker Hill consumed the building above.

Archaeological evidence shows that the residents of Charlestown filled the foundation of the tavern by pushing soils from the surrounding area into the open hole and on top of the charred remains of the building. In 1788 the townspeople voted never again to build on the land that once held the Three Cranes Tavern. They capped the property with grass and created an open marketplace.[4] In the twentieth century, the market was reduced in size. The streets encroached on the town square, as the raised highway stretched across the landscape and a parking lot was built in part of the former tavern yard. Finally, the threat of imminent destruction of the entire area by the Big Dig tunnel triggered the need for a massive archaeological survey. This remarkable archaeological discovery is one of the earliest structures that may possibly survive from the first European settlement in Boston, and the fact that even a portion of it outlasted redevelopment as a tavern, the fighting of the Revolutionary War, and the urbanization of Charlestown in the nineteenth and twentieth centuries is critical proof of the potential preservation of early sites in Boston.

10. Portuguese Plate

1638–1656 | James Garrett Site, Charlestown

Although Boston was a major city in the seventeenth century, extensive development and the general lack of artifacts found on early sites have resulted in relatively few seventeenth-century sites being excavated in town. One exception is the James Garrett site, located near the USS *Constitution* dock in the Charlestown neighborhood of Boston.

James Garrett was a sea captain who in 1638 built his home on the shore of Charlestown, in sight of the wharfs and docks (figure 10.1). He and his wife rode out the tumult of the English civil war (1642–1651) in the relative quiet of this town north of Boston, returning to England in 1656.[1] Upon their departure, their house was demolished and the foundation filled.

Archaeologists excavating along Water Street in the 1980s in connection with the Big Dig survey encountered the foundation of Garrett's home in an area dense with foundations of nineteenth- and twentieth-century industrial buildings.[2] Like so many other sites from this period, mere chance prevented the exact location of the foundation from being destroyed by development while it sat dormant for over 300 years. Unlike the Great House and many other contemporary sites, the Garrett site contained a remarkably dense and diverse assemblage of artifacts representing the period between the house's construction and demolition (1638–1656), including a remarkable international assemblage of ceramics. The collection as a whole represents one of the largest and most diverse archaeological assemblages from an early seventeenth-century site in New England.

FIGURE 10.1
View of Charlestown north of Boston in a 1694 map (Fraquelin 1693; image courtesy of the Norman B. Leventhal Map Center at the Boston Public Library).

Garrett likely traveled through the Azores, a tiny chain of islands off the coast of Portugal, which owns them. Of the 335 ceramic vessels (dishes, plates, cups, and so on) identified at the Garrett site, 20 percent were made in Portugal.[3] The plate shown in the main photo depicts the Portuguese coat of arms. These popular dishes with bold blue decorations were themselves Portuguese copies of Wan-Li-style Ming Dynasty Chinese porcelain. The great number of Portuguese vessels found at the Garrett site would have been expensive to collect, but ceramics of this kind would have been available in any port where Portuguese merchants traded.

As a captain, Garrett had direct access to goods and ports of call around the Atlantic, as is very clear from the remarkable assemblage

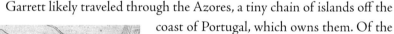

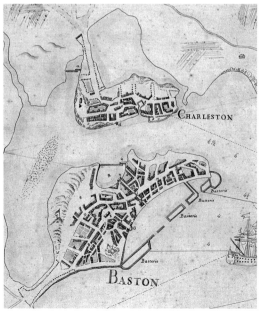

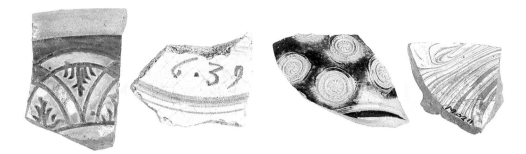

of personal and trade items found in his house. The fragment of tin glaze shown in figure 10.2 conveniently contains the date "1639," which coincides with the date when Garrett and his wife first built their house. Perhaps this plate commemorates their new home, or perhaps it was just one of the many German, English, Dutch, Portuguese, and Spanish luxury goods the wealthy Garrett family was able to acquire.

The seventeenth-century world was smaller than many think, and odd artifacts from abroad were not limited to overseas. Nearly one hundred red-clay earthenware tobacco pipes from the mid-Atlantic colonies around Virginia were found at Garrett's home. These pipes are incredibly rare in Boston, only about a dozen others being known from all other Boston sites combined. The rarity of these pipes, coupled with their huge numbers at the site, indicates that Garrett was not only an avid smoker, but also likely made regular visits to the southern colonies as part of his normal business travels. Although there are no records of what types of cargo Garrett transported, we know he had a worldly existence and great mobility, thanks to broad-reaching networks of communication among people and of trade in goods in the early seventeenth century. James Garrett was killed when his ship sank somewhere in the Atlantic Ocean in 1657.

FIGURE 10.2 Selection of seventeenth-century ceramics from James Garrett's house, including examples from Germany, Italy, and England.

II. Chamber Pot

1660–1715 | Katherine Nanny Naylor Privy, North End

In 1994, archaeologists from the now-defunct Office of Public Archaeology at Boston University were conducting the archaeological survey on a parcel of land called the Cross Street Back Lot in an area that had once been part of the North End but at the time was dominated by the massive elevated highway that once sliced through downtown Boston. After removing the parking lot under the highway, they found an area approximately fifteen feet square that had somehow managed to escape being disturbed by construction for hundreds of years. Not expecting to find much more than the rear yard of an old house, the archaeologists instead quickly uncovered an eight-and-a-half by five-foot rectangle of brick (figure 11.1). Having excavated numerous similar structures throughout Boston pertaining to its archaeology before the Big Dig, the archaeologists immediately realized they had encountered the vault of a privy—an outhouse.[1]

Archaeologists returned later to carefully excavate layer after layer of rubble, human feces, and massive quantities of food and household refuse dumped in the privy. When completed, the vault measured nearly six feet in depth and contained artifacts dating to the mid-1650s.

Like all good archaeologists, the ones on this particular project had done their homework and already knew about all the previous owners of the parcel they were excavating. Although it was impossible to tell prior to excavation which owner the privy was associated with, by the time they had finished, they knew they could unequivocally link the privy and its contents to Katherine Nanny Naylor and her family, who lived on the site from about 1650 to nearly 1700.[2]

FIGURE 11.1
View of the Katherine Nanny Naylor privy at the start of the archaeological excavation (photo courtesy of John Milner Associates, Inc.).

Robert Nanny left England in 1635 at the age of twenty-two, arriving in Boston by way of New Hampshire sometime after 1649. He married thirty-nine-year-old Katherine Wheelwright sometime between 1646 and 1653, and they settled into a one-acre property on Ann Street near the center of Boston.[3] Katherine and Robert had eight children; however, only two survived past infancy. Before Robert died in 1664, he amassed sizable wealth as a successful merchant maintaining a large estate in Barbados remotely, from his home in Boston.

Robert left his estate to Katherine for the benefit of their young children. By 1668, Katherine had remarried Edward Naylor, also a Caribbean merchant.[4] Although the couple produced two children, their relationship was far from happy. In 1671, Katherine filed a petition in the Massachusetts General Court for a divorce from Edward, citing Edward's physical abuse and adulterous actions (see artifact 15 for more details).

Katherine was granted a divorce, the first in Massachusetts's history, and Edward was banished from the colony. Katherine remained in the home with her four surviving children and her servants until she moved, alone, to Charlestown. She spent her remaining years in the home of a friend, keeping house there until her death in 1715.[5]

FIGURE 11.2
Profile of Katherine Nanny Naylor privy showing layers of deposits (Cook and Balicki 1996, 151; image courtesy of John Milner Associates, Inc.).

While living at the Ann Street property, Katherine and her family contributed to the outhouse in several ways. First, the obvious contents resulting from normal use of the privy as a bathroom—both as direct deposits and as secondary deposits—the contents of chamber pots (indoor lidded pots used for toilets). Some of these chamber pots ended up in the privy themselves, such as the one shown in the main photo. The remaining contents of the privy were mostly household waste deposited deliberately in the privy layer by layer (figure 11.2) to clean up space and generally make waste disappear.

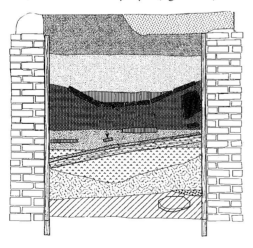

Obviously, Katherine and her family never suspected that their outhouse would one day become the center of scientific study. Thus, they never attempted to "edit" the objects that went into the privy, allowing for an unabridged insight into the daily lives of this family. To emphasize the significance that this single privy has on the early archaeological history of Boston, artifact numbers 10–19 were all found in Katherine's privy and represent a remarkable and personal story of an incredible woman and her family.

12. Whipworm Egg

1660–1715 | Katherine Nanny Naylor's Privy, North End

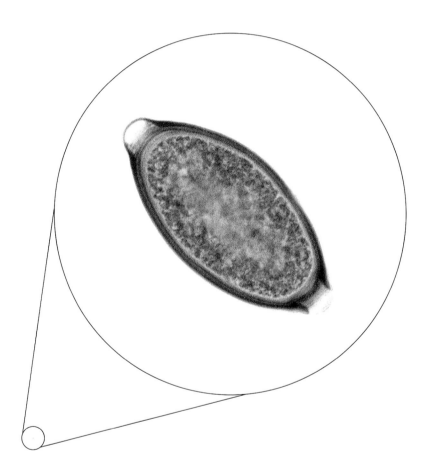

(Mills 2013; image arrangement by author).

Seventeenth-century Boston was not a particularly clean place to live. During this period, ministers were the primary health providers; they treated their patients with prayer, bloodletting, and quack medicinal remedies. Medicine arose as a profession during the late seventeenth century, although doctors' practices were far from improved. In general, most diseases and illnesses were blamed on miasmas—bad odors—and in reaction to this "threat," a law was passed in Boston in 1701 requiring that privies be located more than twelve feet from a road or that their vaults be dug to a depth of six feet to prevent the odors they contained from affecting the health of passersby.[1]

Worry about sickness probably played a secondary role to the general desire to not smell the contents of privies. Until the late 1800s, just about every property in Boston had an outhouse in the backyard, and these can almost always be found as far as possible from the main house. Katherine's privy was no exception; it was located in the corner of her property against the southern and western boundaries of her land.[2]

The presence of fecal matter and the lack of handwashing led to the spread of several disease-causing parasites. The lumpy round eggs of the roundworm and the football-shaped eggs of the whipworm were common in the fecal matter found in Katherine's and other privies excavated before the Big Dig. In great enough concentrations, these animals (figure 12.1) can produce anemia and stomach ailments, including nausea, vomiting, and bloody diarrhea, which aided in the spread of the disease. It is more than likely that the vast majority of seventeenth-century inhabitants of Boston, regardless of their social status or wealth, suffered sustained infestations of bowel parasites.

Found within the privy were not only the causes of discomfort but also their treatments. Folk and home remedies were nearly identical to "professional" medicine during the seventeenth century. Peaches, whose pits were found by the thousands, and *Chenopodium* seeds (similar to quinoa) were found, both of which were documented in period texts as worm expellants. Cherry pits

FIGURE 12.1
Trichuris
(whipworm)
parasite (Bremser
1822, XIX plate 1).

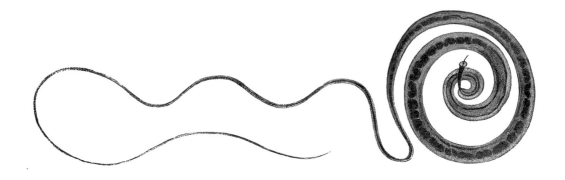

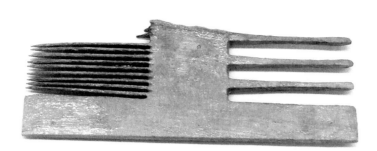

and hawthorn, pepper, dock, pokeweed, and mustard seeds were also found by the hundreds in Katherine's privy. Although many of these could have been eaten as normal foodstuffs, they were also believed at the time to treat fever, worms, headaches, hemorrhoids, and constipation.[3]

Lice, another parasite, were also a constant concern in colonial Boston (and later, too). Lice have been plaguing humans about as long as there have been humans to plague. Egyptians were known to shave their heads and wear wigs to avoid lice, and lice combs have changed little in thousands of years.[4]

Pediculosis, the infestation of humans by lice, begins when adult lice come in contact with head or body hair and lay eggs, which then hatch. Adult lice feed on humans by piercing their skin and drinking blood, causing an irritating itch. Nits and eggs are removed by combs with tightly spaced tines (figure 12.2). Although their materials change—we find bone lice combs in the seventeenth and eighteenth centuries and plastic ones in the nineteenth century, for example—they remain remarkably consistent in form.

It is easy to view parasites as signs of filth and poor living conditions in seventeenth-century Boston, but one must remember that there was little to no infrastructure in existence to treat the causes of stomach bugs and lice, only remedies to treat the symptoms. The Naylor household lived in relative comfort, with many luxury goods not affordable to their neighbors, but everyone in Boston would have suffered relatively equally from these personal plagues.

13. Sleeve

1660–1715 | Katherine Nanny Naylor's Privy, North End

FIGURE 13.1

Painting of Boston
children contempo-
rary with Katherine
Nanny Naylor's
family. Freake-Gibbs
Painter [attrib.],
American, active
1670, *David, Joanna,
and Abigail Mason*,
1670, oil on canvas,
39½ × 42½ in. (Fine
Arts Museums of
San Francisco, gift of
Mr. and Mrs. John
D. Rockefeller III,
1979.7.3.)

Although many of the complex and frustrating aspects of modern life that
exist today did not exist in the seventeenth century, that does not mean that
seventeenth-century Boston life was any less complex and diverse—just
different. Under puritanical laws, Boston women were legally subordinate to
men.[1] When underage, women were considered their father's property until
they married, at which point they were incorporated into all that was legally
considered their husband's property. When a man died, his wife could be
given his property in a will, but if he did not make explicit that the money
was for the benefit of their children (if they had any), the money and belongings deeded to a woman would become the property of a man upon her
remarrying. This could compel a woman to make a choice either to remain
unmarried indefinitely (which would theoretically include celibacy, because
public relationships were considered immoral without marriage) or to allow
her possessions to be transferred to her future husband. As of this writing,
adultery and premarital sex are still listed as illegal according to Massachusetts
General Laws, part IV, title I, chapter 272, sections 14 and 18.

Despite legal subordination to men and overall oppressive legal structures,
seventeenth-century women in Boston played critical roles in society. Pri-

FIGURE 13.2
Detail of
seventeenth-
century marigold
seed embedded
in silk sleeve.

marily, women were homemakers and rearers of children (figure 13.1). Many of the wealthier residents of seventeenth-century Boston, Katherine Nanny Naylor included, were able to hire servants or purchase black or Native slaves to support the household. Although unequal, women were legally allowed to own property, and while they were single were considered their own legal entity. After the death of her first husband and divorce of her second, Katherine Nanny Naylor remained in her home and kept her wealth and possessions, while running her household as a single woman. Property ownership was not limited to wealthy white English settlers. Zipporah Potter, a black woman born free to slaves in the mid-1640s, was able to purchase and own property as a single woman.[2]

Many women worked alongside men, either their husbands or hired help. Male business owners were often assisted by their wives, and many women chose to run businesses independently upon the death of their husbands, although doing so required that they remain unmarried. Many men in commerce and trade were away on boats for significant portions of the year. This resulted in their wives' settling many legal issues between men in their absence, and it was not uncommon for two women to negotiate business and land transactions together on behalf of their respective husbands.[3]

At home, many women were professionals in the domestic arts: sewing, cooking, and care of the home.[4] These were skills critical to the health and well-being of a family, because most food and clothing was made at home. Katherine's privy, despite the fact that she was married during its use, had a disproportionately large number of artifacts that can be associated with women and the domestic arts, such as pins, a needle case, thimbles, a bobbin for thread, and a silk sleeve of a woman's top (main photo and figure 13.2) that was likely made by Katherine or her daughters from supplies purchased downtown.

The sleeve shown in the main photo is made of fine silk, sadly stained by hundreds of years in a privy, with a carefully finished cuff. The fabric used in this garment was imported, as was the thread used to finish it. It is possible that the thread used in the cuff was once spun around a wooden spool that was also recovered from the same privy, and sewn using a needle that was once inside a bone needle case from the privy. Katherine's privy shows that her particular clothing exceeded Puritan standards, with decorative trims and elements that would have been very visual and consciously created signs of her relative wealth.

The remarkable preservation of the moist anaerobic environment of Katherine's outhouse has allowed us to analyze these artifacts, which often do not survive from the colonial era. So many of the mundane objects of everyday life that would have a played major role in the household do not survive the passage of nearly 400 years, simply because their plainness and normalcy do not seem to warrant special attention. Because such everyday items were not saved, these ordinary objects are lost, and archaeologists are tasked with reconstructing daily life from artifacts that rarely make it into the written record.

With Edward being gone so long at sea, and later having been banished from the house, it was the occupants of the house—Katherine; her son Samuel; her three daughters, Mary, Tabitha, and Lydia; and their female servant—that likely contributed these goods to the privy. The presence of so many women in the house is clearly indicated by the presence of numerous items associated directly with women's work in the home, including more than 150 fragments of silk and wool.[5]

14. Bowling Ball

1660–1715 | Katherine Nanny Naylor's Privy, North End

Seventeenth-century Bostonians were much more accustomed to family tragedy than people are today; many children died at a young age, sickness was common, family members were away for extended periods of time, and so on. However, this did not mean that fun was not part of life in Boston—notwithstanding Puritan laws.

Archaeologists excavating the privy of Katherine Nanny Naylor recovered the round wooden object shown in the main photo.[1] At first, they did not know what they had found. It measures approximately five inches across, but is narrower in cross-section, as shown in the side view in figure 14.1. In other words, it is more wheel-shaped than sphere-shaped.

The person that milled the ball sometime in the mid- to late 1600s would have made it on a lathe. During this time, all machinery would have been hand-cranked or foot-powered in large contraptions that allowed the crafts-person to carve the object while powering the machine with their own ex-tremities or through the use of slave or servant labor. They carved concentric circles on the two flat sides of the ball and hollowed out the center.

When it was first encountered, archaeologists thought they had uncovered a large decorative newel post finial, the decorative top found on the end-post of a staircase rail-ing. Further research revealed that the object was in fact a bowling ball. During the seventeenth century, a clandestine pastime was the playing of boules or lawn bowling. Rules changed regularly, but the essential game consisted of rolling a set of similarly shaped balls toward a smaller and previ-ously thrown ball called a *jack*, to see who could get closest. Jacks were typically white, roughly the size of a cue ball, and usually made of painted wood or white stone. The central hole in the wooden bowling ball held a metal weight, prob-ably lead. These weights created centrifugal force, providing stability in the wheel-shaped ball and allowing the ball to go farther with less effort. It is highly likely that this insert was removed and recycled before the ball was discarded, because lead was almost never thrown away. A slightly flattened portion on the ball's edge was caused by the wood splitting at a growth ring. This damage may account for its final disposal.

FIGURE 14.1
Side view of wooden bowling ball.

Lawn bowling has been a popular sport since the thirteenth century, no doubt because of its simple rules, its basic equipment, and the relative ease of finding a playing spot. The game of boules or lawn bowling is still a popular

FIGURE 14.2
Detail of 1728
Boston map show-
ing the location of
bowling green in
today's West End
neighborhood (Bur-
gis 1728; map cour-
tesy of the Norman
B. Leventhal Map
Center at the Boston
Public Library).

sport around the world, and the style of balls is nearly identical to that of the wooden one uncovered in Katherine's privy.

Intriguingly, the game of lawn bowling was banned in the late seventeenth century under Puritan laws that often went against public displays of joy. It is rather difficult to play the game out of the public view, because of the need for fairly large open spaces. Perhaps in the spirit of the sumptuary laws that allowed certain affluent people to be more flamboyant in their appearance, Katherine's family and similarly wealthy families may have been afforded exceptions to the rules as a result of their position in society. It's amazing how little has changed over time! By the early 1700s, it is clear that lawn bowling had become an accepted public activity. Early eighteenth-century maps indicate the presence of a lawn-bowling green in what is today's West End (figure 14.2), and there is even a commemorative plaque in place today indicating its former location.

This bowling ball is the oldest one ever found in the western hemisphere.[2]

15. Plate

1660–1715 | Katherine Nanny Naylor's Privy, North End

Katherine Nanny Naylor was known to historians prior to the archaeological survey on her property. In fact, she will forever be known as the first woman in Massachusetts to legally divorce her husband. The privy that was uncovered during the archaeological survey before the Big Dig dates to a period in Katherine's life when she was living in the home left to her by her first husband with her new husband, Edward Naylor, their two girls, two children from her previous marriage, and at least two house servants who were not slaves.[1]

Though legally subordinate to their husbands, women still had a legal voice, were able to file claims in court, and could testify on their own behalf. Katherine took full advantage of these legal rights in Puritan Boston (figure 15.1).

Her life with Edward was not a happy one. The exact details of the years leading up to her divorce from Edward in 1671 are discussed in her signed testimony, shown in figure 15.1. Katherine cites numerous examples of physical abuse and violence at the hands of Edward, including his throwing of an "earthen platter" at her, perhaps the broken plate from Katherine's privy shown in the main image, and forcing a bedridden Katherine into attending a party immediately after giving birth, despite the pleas that he not do so from both Katherine and her maid. Katherine also states that Edward repeatedly threw either Lydia (age three) or Tabitha (age five) to the floor one night and then kicked Tabitha down a flight of stairs.[2]

Edward's adulterous behavior was also detailed in court, with twenty-five witnesses called to testify against him. For example, a pregnant Mary Read, one of Katherine and Edward's servants, was seen traveling northbound with Edward. Mary later gave birth in New Hampshire and told her midwives and testified in court that Edward was the father. Several local innkeepers also testified in support of Mary's claims, stating they had seen Edward and Mary together in their businesses. Another servant, Mary Moore, was also called out by innkeepers as having frequented inns with Edward, and a third servant, Hannah Allen, eighteen, testified that Edward had attempted to kiss and seduce her before she ran from him. Hannah concluded that Edward was too drunk at the time to prevent her escape or to follow her.[3]

The trial culminated with Katherine testifying that after drinking beer, she fell very ill. Jemima Bisse, a neighbor, was brought in to testify that Mary Read had visited her to purchase henbane, a poisonous herb, just before Katherine fell ill.[4] The accusation was that Mary had attempted, as her illegitimate pregnancy became more visible, to murder Katherine. It seems that even though these events occurred in seventeenth-century Puritan Boston, people will still be people, no matter the century.

Edward was found guilty of "inhumane carriage and several cruelties in abusing his wife and children," "uncivil carriage," and fornication with Mary Read, and was banished from the colony. Katherine continued to live in her home as a single woman with her remaining children. In 1700, Katherine moved to Charlestown, where she lived with an unrelated couple. Upon her death in 1715, her property on Ann Street was willed to her living daughters Lydia and Tabitha.[5]

16. Child's Shoe

1660–1715 | Katherine Nanny Naylor's Privy, North End

For many children in seventeenth-century Boston, the greatest challenge in life was surviving childhood. Statistics show that 12 percent of children born in the seventeenth century would die in the first year of life. More than one-third would die by the age of six, and six out of every ten children born were dead by the age of sixteen.[1] These statistics were for New England as a whole, so the odds would have been worse for urban children in downtown Boston, who were less able than their rural counterparts to avoid polluted water, human waste, and interaction with other people, all of which increased the spread of disease.

The average woman in New England during this period would have given birth to at least eight children, and urban areas would have had higher death rates.[2] Katherine Nanny Naylor is recorded as having had ten children with both her husbands, and only four survived.

Archaeological excavations in Katherine's privy revealed numerous shoes, two of which can be associated with children.[3] The high heel of one shoe (figures 16.1 and 16.2) is intact and shows the layers of dense leather used to create the lift. Such heels not only would have been fashionable and provided the child a bit of height gain, but also would have raised the child's foot slightly above the soil and muck common in Boston's streets. Because smells (miasmas) were believed to cause disease, every possible way to protect children, such as limiting direct contact with smelly substances, would have been employed. It is not possible to determine which of her children wore this shoe, but its remarkable preservation in the anaerobic environment of the privy provides a deeply personal glimpse of a childhood much more fraught with challenges than today.

Children who survived birth and infancy were tasked with many daily activities. In more rural areas, children would begin farm-related chores at a very young age. The lack of legal birth control meant that families could become quite large, which helped with tasks at home. Women with many children were looked upon with great awe and respect in Puritan Boston be-cause childbirth was an extremely risky venture and many children died young. A woman with a large family was certainly doing something right!

As nearly every aspect of daily life in the seventeenth century required self-reliance, children served important roles in daily

FIGURE 16.1
Detail of late seventeenth-century children's shoes from artifact 13. Freake-Gibbs Painter [attrib.], American, active 1670, *David, Joanna, and Abigail Mason*, 1670, oil on canvas 39½ × 42½ in. (Fine Arts Museums of San Francisco, gift of Mr. and Mrs. John D. Rockefeller III, 1979.7.3.)

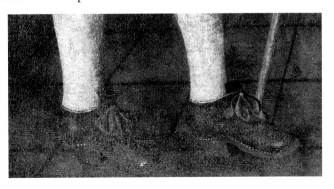

tasks. Many families living in the urban center of Boston had only enough yard space for a pig at best, and laws prevented the keeping of cattle outside common areas. Children would have been responsible for the upkeep of the pig yard, cleaning, running errands, and some cooking. There is little doubt that the least enjoyable task was the daily emptying of the nightly contributions from the chamber pot into the privy. Girls would have begun the training for adulthood at a young age by taking care of the younger members of the family, sewing, and learning all the other skills they would need when they had their own house to manage and family to care for.

Unlike some areas in Europe and some of the other colonies, the settlement in Boston did not differentiate widely between the rich and the poor. In less urban areas, wealthy families like Katherine's would have been able to physically remove themselves and their children from some of the risks associated with childhood, but because rich and poor often lived side by side and shared resources such as water in seventeenth-century Boston, all Bostonians were similarly affected by disease.

17. Fruit Pits

1660–1715 | Katherine Nanny Naylor's Privy, North End

Urban centers such as Boston in the seventeenth century had relatively dense settlements that made their residents unable to sustain themselves on food that they grew on their own land. This created a daily challenge, because their food had to be purchased or gathered elsewhere and brought to the home before being processed. Boston received its food resources from various sources: the sea, small farms downtown, larger farms in Roxbury and Dorchester, domestic farm animals, and some wild animals hunted in the more rural areas.

Merchants in the seventeenth century did not have a central marketplace to sell their goods—that came with the construction of Faneuil Hall in 1742. Instead, carts were loaded with goods from boats, farms, and local artisans and traversed the city selling their merchandise directly to individuals and businesses.

The late seventeenth-century privy at Katherine Nanny Naylor's family home offered excellent preservation of organic materials because of its saturated and anaerobic environment, which left behind over 9,000 pieces of bone that had been tossed into the privy from the kitchen. In general, the Puritan Boston diet was high in fat and low in spices, and it contained an abundance of beef.[1] Whereas Katherine's family's diet generally follows these documented ideas, the archaeological materials demonstrate a much more diverse and complete picture of Boston's early colonial diet.

FIGURE 17.1 Complete late seventeenth-century earthenware pot excavated from the privy of Katherine Nanny Naylor.

The vast majority of the food remains in the privy were from cattle, followed by sheep and pig. In the lowest level of the privy, an entire intact juvenile pig skeleton (artifact 18, figure 18.2) was found just under a capping layer.[2] It is believed that this pig likely died of disease in the mid- to late seventeenth century and Katherine's family buried it whole in the privy and covered it with clay to prevent disease and smell. Although Katherine had a yard, it was only large enough to keep one or two pigs to eat food waste and to allow for the growing of some food. This pig was likely one she had in her yard.

That cows were butchered nearby is indicated by the fact that head and feet were found in the privy. These parts would most likely not have been purchased by this relatively wealthy family, so it is likely the butchering may have occurred in or near the yard. Cows, pigs, and sheep were not the only meats available; the privy also showed that Katherine and her family ate other animals, including lobster, various fish, goose, chicken, passenger pigeon (now extinct), deer, and duck.[3]

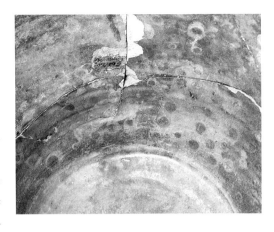

Meat was not the only component of their diet; plants played a significant role for both food and medicine. In total, thirty-two different types of seeds were found in the privy, some deposited as kitchen waste and others passed through the family's digestive system. These plants include raspberry, strawberry, blueberry, huckleberry, squash, grape, olive, pear, hawthorn, elderberry, pepper, chestnut, walnut, mustard, carrot, and stone fruit (peaches, plums, and cherries). Stone fruit were well represented; in fact, archaeologists recovered an entire pot that once contained cherries as well as over 250,000 peach, plum, and cherry pits in a privy that measured just 5 × 8 × 6 feet[4] (figure 17.1 and 17.2).

Although we are not exactly sure what specifically Katherine was doing with these fruits, she and many other households in Boston were probably making fruit pies and preserves. One potential use for massive quantities of cherries and other stone fruit is cherry bounce or cherry wine, two alcoholic beverages that could be made in reused wine bottles in one's basement (which was illegal). A complete, large ceramic jar was found that contained numerous pits and evidence of spoilage prior to deposition, which shows that one batch of fruit brought to the house may have spoiled so badly before use that it and the usable pot it was kept in were thrown out in the privy.

While the Naylor family may have struggled with the hazards of disease from food handling and improper waste disposal, their privy clearly documents that the diet of seventeenth-century Bostonians was diverse, full of fresh fruit, and, at least in this household, included plenty of meat.

18. Bellarmine Bottle

1660–1715 | Katherine Nanny Naylor's Privy, North End

Puritan customs discouraged the ostentatious display of wealth because it distracted from religious pursuits and created tension between individuals. In seventeenth-century Boston, wealthy and poor people lived in relatively the same location within house lots that did not vary to a great extent in size on the relatively small Shawmut peninsula. In additional, many of the houses were similar in size and height: wood was the prominent building material, brick or stone being used for chimneys and thatch or shake for roofs. At street level, it would have been relatively difficult to determine who was wealthy and who was poor simply by walking down the streets of Boston and viewing homes.

That did not mean, however, that egalitarianism ruled. In fact, by the end of the seventeenth century, there were many Boston merchants with great wealth. Laws passed in the early 1700s, including the Treaty of Utrecht, brought some stability to trade relationships between the West and Europe and resulted in a dramatic increase in trade and wealth for Boston merchants. In 1651, the Massachusetts General Court passed a series of clothing-related sumptuary laws that specifically forbade the wearing of particular types of clothing unless the wearer possessed certain educational and financial standards (see artifact 19 for a longer discussion of wealth and clothing). One of the few places where wealth was visible was in the dinnerware of the residents of the house.

Dinner in the Naylor residence would have been similar to dinner in a fifteenth- or sixteenth-century medieval house in England. On poorer families' tables, larger vessels would have held food for the entire family, and plates would have been wood or pewter and modest in appearance. Since relatively few ceramics were made locally in the seventeenth century and Boston was one of the most important ports of global trade, the tableware in the home of a wealthy family like the Naylors would typically have included plates from England, Portugal, and the Netherlands; glasses from Italy and Germany; bottles and jugs from Germany (main photo and figure 18.1); serving dishes from Italy; and storage containers from Spain. Archaeologists were able to corroborate the historic record of Katherine's wealth from the more expensive cuts of meat that her family ate, the expensive dishes she used, and the relative number of dishes found in the privy.[1]

Katherine's plates were made mostly in England and the Netherlands, large platters being the most

FIGURE 18.1 Detail of the grotesque face on the Bellarmine bottle.

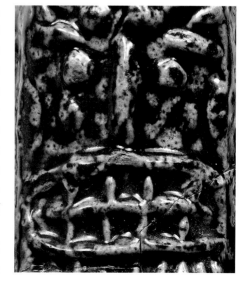

common form (artifact 15 shows a portion of one of these). These plates were typically decorated in blue cobalt on white backgrounds, although other decorations were also found. During this period, a matched set of dishes and drinking cups was almost unheard of, and individual vessels were purchase on an as-needed basis.

Their glassware included expensive imported Venetian and German-styled glassware with flamboyant colorful and decorative elements that went completely against the modesty of Puritan Boston.[2] It is clear that Katherine and her family were not ashamed to exhibit their relative wealth. The broad range of expensive goods available from around the globe and their own backyard (as evidenced by the pig skeleton) speaks to the complex and widespread networks of trade already in existence in the Atlantic in the seventeenth century and the ability of the city's new merchants, like Katherine's husbands, to take the goods produced in Boston (mainly fish, wood, rum, and salt pork) and incorporate their trade into these existing networks. As a result, a plethora of exotic goods were available to the residents of Boston, to an extent that nearly rivals the present.

19. Lace

1660–1715 | Katherine Nanny Naylor's Privy, North End

FIGURE 19.1

FIGURE 19.1
Detail of
seventeenth-
century lace from
Katherine Nanny
Naylor's privy.

As a wealthy family, Katherine and her children were afforded luxuries that were legally unavailable to others. While Puritan practice stressed modesty of the whole, sumptuary laws passed in 1651 explicitly stated that certain pieces of clothing were allowed only for certain people. These laws were created after the Massachusetts court grew tired of Bostonians' ignoring the individual orders and declarations regarding clothing choices. Acknowledging the "blindness of men's minds and the stubbornness of their wills," the members of the court still felt it their duty to express their "utter detestation and dislike" of poor people wearing "the garb [of] gentlem[e]n," laying out a list of explicit laws to ensure "sober and moderate" clothing of the public.[1]

For example, buttons and lace with gold or silver thread were allowed to be worn only by those who possessed an estate valued at more than 200 pounds or those who had received advanced formal education. Points at knees, boots that exceeded the height of the knee, silk hoods, scarves, bone lace (figure 19.1), and ribbons (which were deemed one of the worst offenses) were also banned unless you met the requirement for wealth or education. Moreover, it was the right and responsibility of the town's selectmen to judge residents of Boston at a glance and determine whether the wearers of such goods met these socioeconomic standards. All public officers were completely exempt from these rules, of course, as were people who came from formerly wealthy families but were now financially below grade.

Some of the most obvious signs of Katherine's wealth are the silk lace with silver threads, the ribbons, and the overall quality of clothing materials excavated from her privy. Such items speak to the Naylor family's financial ability to work above and around these Puritan rules simply because they were wealthy, although they likely still made and mended some of their own clothes (figure 19.2). As shown by artifact 14, the lawn bowling ball, this extended not just to clothing but to leisure as well.

Walking down the street in seventeenth-century Boston, you would see men clothed in loose-fitting long white shirts tucked into breeches that buttoned at the knee. Socks and leather shoes like those found in Katherine's privy would be found on most feet, and coats and hats completed the look.

Relatively few pieces of men's and children's clothing were found in the privy. This is probably because over time the children's clothing would have been reused and repaired for each new child, thus making the tossing out of children's clothing rarer than disposal of adult clothing. For Edward and his son, besides being outnumbered by women at least three to one, his merchant position in Boston's economy coupled with his multiacre estate in Barbados, which he kept throughout his marriage with Katherine, both meant that he was away from his home in Boston for lengthy periods of time. One would expect that on Edward's return home from a journey, his old or worn-out clothing would be discarded and replaced with new duds, but perhaps the old clothes were reused or disposed of on his journeys.

Women of this period would have worn loose-fitting dress-like undergarments with petticoats forming broad skirts over and around their waist and legs. Jackets, coats, and capes allowed them to venture outdoors during the cold weather, and wool socks protected their feet inside leather shoes.

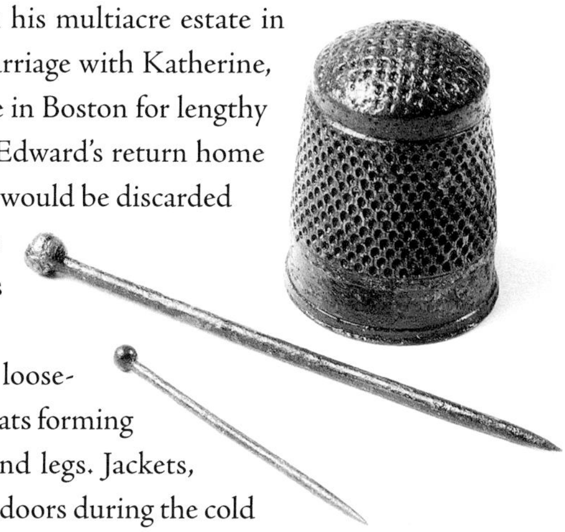

FIGURE 19.2 Seventeenth-century thimble and pins excavated from Katherine Nanny Naylor's privy.

20. Red-Clay Pipe

Circa 1720 | John Carnes Site, North End

Although Boston was a leader in the antislavery movement in the nineteenth century, slavery was legal and common in Boston from its founding until it was banned in 1783. In fact, Massachusetts was the first colony to legalize slavery in 1641, and the port of Boston was the center of the New England slave trade throughout the seventeenth and eighteenth centuries. Town Dock (where Faneuil Hall is now located) and other nearby docks and wharves served as places to unload captured Africans and Native Americans and sell them on the open market as chattel (personal property).

Puritan law treated slaves in the same manner as bound domestic servants. Bound domestic servants were typically younger boys and girls from lower-income white families who were sent to wealthier families or businesses as servants or apprentices for a certain period of years. Indentured servitude also was a commonplace form of repayment by those who traveled from Europe on borrowed money, at least until their debts were paid, to those who paid for their transportation. Legal treatment allowed for slaves and other servants to sue their owners for mistreatment and abuse, but the biggest difference between slaves and bound servants was that indentured servants and children were usually bound to service by themselves or their family for set periods of time, whereas slaves were sold into servitude unwillingly, usually for the duration of their lives. Interestingly, in Massachusetts, children of slaves were born free, which allowed individuals like Zipporah Potter, the daughter of a Boston slave, to live as a free woman and purchase property in seventeenth-century Boston. It is important to note that slavery went beyond individuals of African descent to include local Native Americans, who were often forcibly taken to the West Indies to be traded for African slaves and goods (figure 20.1).

FIGURE 20.1 Detail of the base of an earthenware African pipe bowl.

Regardless of their origin, slaves or "servants for life" were bought, sold, taxed as personal property, and transferred to others via wills. Much of the evidence about slaves in Boston comes from these wills. Very few written documents include names and personal information about these individuals; occasionally, however, a slave's name appeared in a will, or the owner made comments regarding the length of time a slave was owned by a family, or his or her age or health. Archaeology is a major source of new historical data regarding these voiceless people who were present in and made significant contributions to Boston's culture and history, yet are not themselves significantly represented in the historic written record, which most consider the main source of historical data. Archaeologists realize that the written record is only part of a much larger history.

Documentary evidence at the site of Katherine Nanny Naylor's home shows that at least fourteen Africans or African Americans lived in at least eight households in the immediate vicinity. During the seventeenth century, Katherine's direct neighbors, the Lake family, had a slave, "Besse," who may

be the "Jemima Bisse" who sold Mary Read the henbane that may have been used to poison Katherine, as mentioned in the discussion of her 1670s divorce trial (artifact 15).[1] This indication points to some knowledge base in herbal medicines within the area surrounding Katherine's home. The likely source was the African slaves who had brought their knowledge of traditional West African herbal remedies to Boston and incorporated local flora into these traditions. The servants of the Naylor household do not appear to have been of African or Native descent.

Many slaves would have been first- or second-generation arrivals who would have brought aspects of their daily lives in their native homes with them. The red-clay pipe shown in the main photograph was found at the neighboring John Carnes site and is of a style associated with West Africa. It could have been brought to Boston by a slave working at the Carnes house, because Carnes himself was not an overseas merchant. While slave owners would have probably discouraged the continuity of slaves' African practices, these nevertheless contribute to the archaeological record.

A brown ceramic pot fragment shown in figure 20.2 is a piece of "colonoware" recovered from Katherine Nanny Naylor's privy. *Colonoware* is a general term referring to ceramics produced by people of African descent in North America using local clay. This ceramic type is closely associated with the mid-Atlantic region of the United States, and the example shown here is the largest fragment of the most complete colonoware vessel recovered in Massachusetts.

PART 3 From Colonist to Rebel
(1700–1775)

As Boston grew, its merchants, craftspeople, sailors, and their families created a quirky yet vibrant city. Growth brought with it a new identity, one that was defined by strength, independence, and resistance. At the turn of the eighteenth century, Cotton Mather referred to Boston as the "Metropolis of the Whole English America."[1] The early eighteenth century in Boston was marked by stability and remarkable economic and physical expansion within the city that transformed the Shawmut peninsula into a bustling economic and social capital bursting at its shoreline seams. The Three Cranes Tavern became a center of Boston culture. Archaeologists excavating prior to the Big Dig rediscovered the 1635–1775 Three Cranes Tavern (shown in an artist's construction here); many of the artifacts discussed in this part were recovered at this site. Stability and prosperity gave Bostonians their own identity and pride, which they could safely credit to their entrepreneurial spirit and work ethic.

By the middle of the eighteenth century, the British Crown began to bristle at the cost of defending the colonies with British treasure, as the colonists filled their own pockets with earnings made possible by this protection. A series of parliamentary acts passed in London attempted to fund the management of the colonies by taxing some of the most popular goods, including molasses, sugar,

Artist's reconstruction of the Three Cranes Tavern (image courtesy of the Public Archaeology Laboratory, Inc.; color added by author).

tea, lead, paper, paint, and lumber. As the largest and most lucrative port in the British colonies, Boston was a leader in the resistance against these acts. The colonists believed that the acts were illegal because the taxpayers did not have representation in Parliament and thus did not have a say when such acts were being discussed and passed, giving rise to the phrase *no taxation without representation*.

As hostilities, anger, and resistance grew in Boston, the Crown responded with military and economic force. This heavy-handed reaction only served to anger Bostonians even more and eventually led to physical clashes and acts of resistance such as the 1770 Boston Massacre and the 1771 Boston Tea Party. Thousands of British troops were sent to resist the rebellion, and Boston stood at the helm of a war that would lead to the creation of a new country.

21. Cat Skeleton

1714–1750 | Three Cranes Tavern, Charlestown

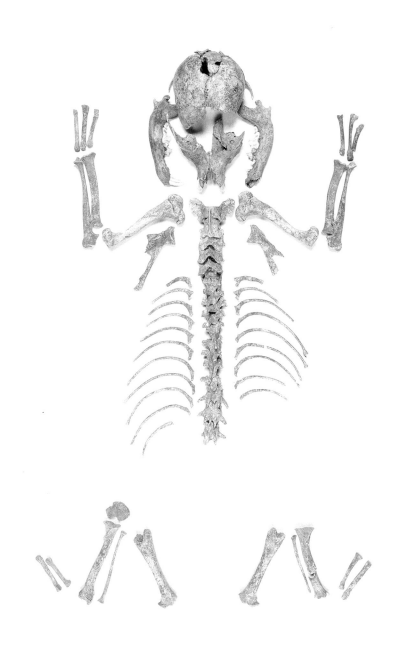

The Salem Witch Trials of the 1690s affected many nearby communities, including Boston. Although most of the related hysteria had died down by the turn of the eighteenth century, trials continued throughout Europe, and "witches" were executed well into the 1790s. While it was eventually made clear that many of the accusations were false, the event exposed a general environment of fear, superstition, and ritual that underlay the religious and social appearances of Puritan Boston.

Archaeologists encounter many artifacts and odd deposits that do not fit standard narratives of the past. Whereas some of these can be explained easily, others become clear only when the same odd occurrences are found in multiple sites. Superstitious behaviors are one of these. A contemporary behavior that would leave an odd archaeological deposit today is the burying of a St. Joseph statue upside down and facing the house when one wants to sell a property. Although the statue is supposed to be removed after the sale, a future archaeologist could come along and find the odd deposit if it is left there. These types of unusual deposits can at first appear to be oddities, but when they are found at multiple sites under similar conditions, archaeologists can build a case for a relatively widespread superstitious behavior.

Today we have the benefit of numerous means of recording our rituals and superstitious behaviors, but in the past, these traditions were often not recorded—even if they were familiar to most people at the time. From the sixteenth through nineteenth centuries, it was a fairly common folk practice to hide a "witch bottle" in homes. These bottles typically were a type of German stoneware called Bellarmine jugs (artifact 18), whose defining characteristic is a bold, grotesque face on the neck of the bottle. The tradition included placing pins, needles, nails, hair, urine, fabric, fingernails, and other objects in a sealed bottle placed near a home's hearth that would protect the occupants from witchcraft and evil spirits, and numerous examples of these odd artifact assemblages in sealed Bellarmine jugs have been found near hearths at seventeenth-century archaeological sites.

One possible ritual interment was encountered during the archaeological dig at the Three Cranes Tavern in Charlestown's City Square site. Beneath the threshold of the main entrance to the building, archaeologists found a small pit.[1] As they excavated the contents, they first encountered a nearly complete earthenware bowl decorated in a style that matched the

FIGURE 21.1
View of puncture and fracture at the rear of a cat skull that occurred at the time of death.

pottery of the Parker potters, who were located across the street (artifact 24). As excavations continued within and around the bowl, the archaeologists began to uncover small bones. These bones appeared to be part of a skeleton of a small cat, and because they were arranged in anatomical order, it was apparent that the cat was buried intact with the bowl. It was possible to date the entire deposit to sometime after 1714, when the Parkers began their company, but before 1750, as that was the date of the deposit that covered the pit.

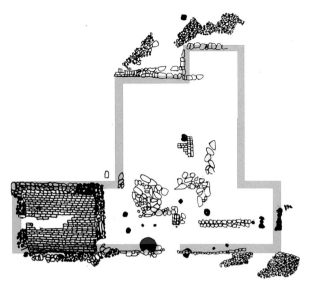

FIGURE 21.2

Plan view of the Three Cranes Tavern showing the building foundation (blue) and circular pit under the threshold (red) where the cat skeleton was located (image courtesy of the Public Archaeology Laboratory, Inc.; color added by author).

The rear of the cat's skull had been struck—around the time of death—with a narrow or pointed object that not only caused a puncture and cracks to the rear of the skull, but appears to have heavily damaged the eye and forehead area of the skull, because these bones were never recovered (figure 21.1). Although it is possible that the cat was deliberately buried as a family pet or casually discarded in a trash pit (cats were not particularly valued or appreciated in the early eighteenth century), it is just as likely that this cat was deliberately killed in a ritual interment at the threshold of the tavern to protect the occupants from supernatural harm (figure 21.2).

During this period it was relatively common to deliberately place cats and other objects, like shoes and dead mice (in the mouth of the cat), within walls, under chimneys, in roofs, and under thresholds as a superstitious ritual to ward off witchcraft, protect the house, and avoid pests.[2] Although many of these behaviors began with folk traditions in Europe, it is clear that they continued to persist in Boston.

22. Whizzer

Circa 1750 | Faneuil Hall, Downtown

As was true in the seventeenth century, children are relatively absent from much of the written historic record in the eighteenth century. Archaeologists are always in search of children's narratives during excavation and analysis, as these are areas in which the lack of written data allows archaeology to shine in its contribution to history. Leisure activities, toys, and games were not limited to children, and gaming pieces (figure 22.1) typically used to play the popular game of Nine Men's Morris (figure 22.2), a cross between tic-tac-toe and checkers, are fairly common on eighteenth-century archaeological sites. Usually the archaeological evidence of children is subtle—a marble here, a fragment of a doll there—and sometimes we find less subtle artifacts, such as a toy with a child's name stamped on it. This artifact is one of those objects.

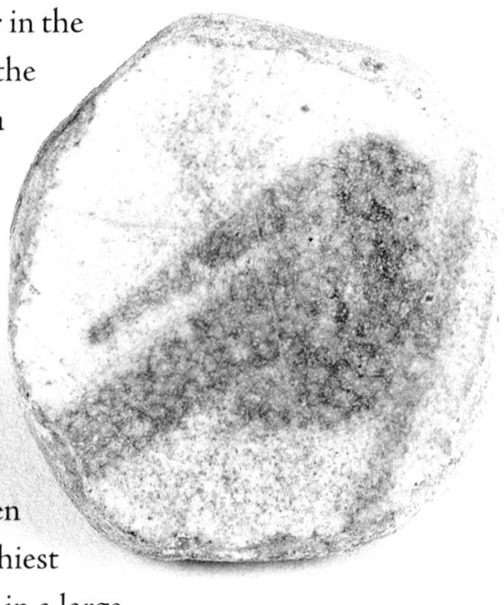

FIGURE 22.1
Eighteenth-century gaming token made from a shard of soft, tin-glazed ceramic with blue decoration that was excavated from the Clough House site in Boston's North End.

This whizzer was likely made from a musket ball that had been hammered flat, leaving not only the hammer marks on the back side of the toy but also the frayed edges of the disk as the lead ball stretched and tore.[1] The two holes in the center allowed a loop of string to pass through them. A person would hold either side of the loop of string with the whizzer in the middle, spin the whizzer around vertically, and then pull the string tight, causing it to spin extremely quickly and creating a "whizzing" sound—surely the height of eighteenth-century entertainment.

This rare artifact is made even more remarkable by the name "Thomas Apthorp" stamped clearly across one side, and the fact that it was found by archaeologists in 2010 during the archaeological survey of the Town Dock, filled in the eighteenth century, alongside Faneuil Hall.[2]

Thomas Apthorp was born in 1741, one of eighteen children of Grizzell Eastwick and Charles Apthorp, one of the wealthiest individuals in Boston. Thomas and his massive family lived in a large home on King Street, now State Street, and attended King's Chapel, where their family filled the entirety of rows 5 and 22.[3] Thomas's father's success as a merchant and slave trader afforded his family many luxury goods, including this customized whizzer, and the changing cultural practices during the middle of the eighteenth century meant that the family was no longer burdened by concern over public modesty. The wealthy of eighteenth-century Boston wanted to make sure everyone knew their status; they did so through their dress, their massive homes, and the goods they bought, and no doubt other Bostonians wanted to emulate them.

Thomas was born just one year before the construction of the first Faneuil Hall in 1742 (the one now standing is a much-enlarged version built in 1805).

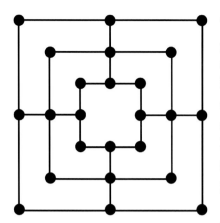

This whizzer, which must have been a valued personal possession of Thomas's, possibly flew into the dock next to Faneuil Hall when the whizzer string broke, or perhaps he accidentally dropped it during a trip to his father's store on merchant's row, which ran along the street that now extends from Faneuil Hall to Quincy Market southward. Not all children were afforded such luxuries, although most other eighteenth-century sites throughout Boston yield evidence of children's toys.

Thomas's father died when the boy was just seventeen years old, but he immediately took over his father's role as paymaster for the British navy, which was stationed in Boston. His role in support of the Crown was not appreciated by rebels, and he was banished from the city as a loyalist in 1778.[4]

23. Porcelain Tea Bowl and Saucer

1762–1775 | Three Cranes Tavern, Charlestown

Chinese porcelain, like this bowl and saucer, was treasured by Bostonians. These thinly potted and delicately painted wares were produced by artisans in China using a secret formula of clays, and heat. Because these pieces were both finely made and needed to be transported via ship to Boston from Canton, China, their cost was greater than that of almost all other forms of ceramic available for sale in Boston at the end of the eighteenth century. Many mariners from Boston made the long journey from the East Coast, around the Horn of Africa, through Indonesia, and into the port of Canton (now Guangzhou), where these delicate ceramics were purchased for import.

The port of Canton was a major center of ceramic trade. Potters would produce these wares in small village kilns, and entire communities would contribute to the mining of the right types of clay and feldspar, throwing the vessels by hand on a potter's wheel, hand-painting the decoration, firing, packaging, and transporting to port each of the millions of vessels like this bowl that eventually made it to America via ports such as Boston.

Boston's Town Dock was located where Faneuil Hall is today. The port would have been the main source of foreign and domestic goods made outside Boston, and archaeological investigations within the foundations of Faneuil Hall documented this trade in the fill of the former dock, which included the

FIGURE 23.1

Eighteenth-century lead seal with impressed sun motif of the manufacturer found during excavations in the former Town Dock next to the Faneuil Hall market.

lead seal shown in figure 23.1. Seals like this would have been used by merchants to mark their goods, much like a logo or brand today.

Ceramics such as the cup and saucer in the main image tell archaeologists about much more than just trade and commerce. These particular vessels were found in the outhouse deposits at the Three Cranes Tavern in Charlestown. As important as the local town hall and courthouse (perhaps even more), the tavern served as the central secular meeting place for the community, where local folks could meet, discuss politics, and eat and visitors from the nearby docks on Charlestown's waterfront were able to purchase a meal, drink, and find temporary lodging.

This and many other ceramic tea wares and tablewares (figure 23.2) were used as part of the services provided to tavern guests. Tea bowls functioned exactly like teacups, except that handles did not become popular on teacups until the nineteenth century. One would expect that a tavern would not serve its guests in the most expensive ceramics available on the market, but it is

apparent from the numerous Chinese porcelain items in the privies of the tavern that its customers enjoyed the use of fine china.

Perhaps Mary Brown, the owner of the Three Cranes at the time, charged more for the services at her tavern and let other taverns in the area (there were many) serve those unable to meet the costs of the finer establishment. What we do know is that Mary did not spare expense for her customers, and they certainly appreciated it, because the tavern, which opened in 1635, lasted 135 years until, at the peak of its popularity, its run was ended by the burning of Charlestown on June 17, 1775.

This burning resulted in the complete destruction of Charlestown, including privy 2. Located by archaeologists in 1985, privy 2 was one of five privies built in the yard of the tavern during its existence and its only privy still in active use during the lead-up to the Revolutionary War. When archaeologists first encountered privy 2, now a square arrangement of stones about four feet across marking the foundation of the outhouse, they found that the upper levels contained the charred and blackened wooden remains of the privy structure that was once located above the privy. This deposit further solidified the interpretation that this privy burned during the Battle of Bunker Hill, thus permanently entombing its contents, including this porcelain tea bowl and saucer.

24. Redware Waster

1715–1760 | Parker-Harris Pottery Site, Charlestown

The fires set by the British during the Battle of Bunker Hill left Charlestown in smoldering ruins. Although the city rebuilt, what was lost was not only the first 150 years of architecture, but also the numerous businesses and industries that never returned. The redware or earthenware industry in Charlestown was one of these industries. At the height of Charlestown's pottery-making endeavors, dozens of individual potters were active along the shoreline of Charlestown. The distinctive kilns used to fire the ceramics, which were either rectangular huts or tall, bottle-shaped chimneys with bulbous bases, would have looked like a line of smoking chimneys along Charlestown's wharves, creating a distinctive view from Boston or the harbor, a visual characteristic that is now gone.

FIGURE 24.1
Waster composed of a fused mug, triangular kiln trivet (used to separate individual vessels in the kiln during firing), and the rim of a chamber pot, indicating that mugs were likely fired within chamber pots at the Parker-Harris pottery site.

During the war, the potters in Charlestown were forced to abandon their kilns and homes and flee abroad, many heading to other towns nearby with strong ceramic industries and numerous family members. When they returned after the war, in some cases years later, they found their expensive infrastructure gone, and often chose to return permanently to their temporary locations, where they could produce pottery without starting from scratch. In many ways, the ceramic industry in Charlestown was one of the reasons the town it flourished; without the ceramics industry, which has been completely forgotten by most today, there would not have been as much of Charlestown to burn.

Charlestown was ideally situated for a ceramics industry. Its three-sided shoreline faced the Charles River, Mystic River, and Boston Harbor. From this point, ships could easily traverse the Mystic, collecting raw clay deposited by the former glacier and exposed by the river cut, and ships could transport finished pottery to nearly any port on the East Coast. The potters concentrated their production directly on the wharves and shores of Charlestown. You can imagine that a fragile commodity like pottery would benefit from traveling the shortest possible distance between production site and transportation ship. Plus, with kilns located along the shore, any out-of-control firing would be more easily doused with seawater.

Things certainly did go wrong in the kilns. The artifact presented in the main photo shows a "waster"—an unfortunate occurrence that resulted when kilns were heated too high or when hot spots formed within the kiln.

Although the pottery in the kiln had to reach a temperature that would partially melt the clay, forming a glassier and harder ceramic, too high a temperature would actually melt the pot, causing it to slump and be unusable (figure 24.1). Near all kilns you will find a pile of wasters, which were discarded because of slumping, discoloring, or breaking in the kiln—any number of things can go wrong when you place hundreds of objects into a closed room and crank the temperature to around 1,000 degrees for a day.

Archaeologists excavating at the Parker-Harris pottery site in Charlestown prior to the Big Dig project (figure 24.2) came across the 1715–1775 waster pile of the Parkers and later the Harrises, two potter families operating out of the same workshop, which contained tens of thousands of fragments of slumped vessels, kiln furniture, and other broken pieces that never made it to the market.[1] The particular example in the main photo has decoration associated with the Parker phase (1715–1760) of the Parker-Harris pottery operation.

The Charlestown ceramics industry was dominated by families of potters, many of whom would intermarry so they could have job security between kiln locations and, in the case of emergency, find refuge and work at a relative's pottery operation in another town. Many businesses were passed from father to son or, in the case of Grace Parker (artifact 25), from husband to wife. Women played a major role in the ceramics industry in Charlestown. Some were potters themselves, as decorators of the final pots; apprentices; or even owners of entire operations.

Six pottery kiln sites were subject to archaeological investigation during the Big Dig surveys. These digs revealed massive quantities of ceramic data on both the production and the consumption of these important pieces of Charlestown history.

25. Parker-Harris Mug

1715–1755 | Parker-Harris Pottery Site, Charlestown

Mugs were prevalent among the artifacts found in the privies located behind the Three Cranes Tavern, perhaps for obvious reasons. Made to hold predetermined volumes (this one holds a quart), mugs at the tavern were formed from several types of ceramics, from lowly redware chamber pots (figure 25.1) to the more expensive white-colored tea wares. Based on the decorations and overall colorings, it is likely that this mug was made next door at the Parker-Harris pottery site, also excavated by archaeologists ahead of the Big Dig, approximately during the 1740s, when the company was owned by Grace Parker, the first female pottery owner in America. Grace was a pivotal figure in the Charlestown neighborhood of Boston. She and her husband, Isaac, founded a pottery in 1714 on the southwestern shore of Charlestown, just across the street from City Square, the site of the Three Cranes Tavern. Grace's husband died in 1742, leaving the business, land, and their mansion to Grace in his will.[1]

Boston's common laws stated that women were able to hold property, but if they married, their property was transferred to their new husbands.[2] This situation left many widowed women with a decision upon the deaths of their husbands: to keep what they had and remain unmarried forever, or marry and have all of their property and control of their estate automatically transferred to their new husband. Grace chose to keep the company she helped build, but in doing so was never able to remarry, despite the struggles she must have faced running a large pottery business. Her business was successful, her family was quite wealthy, and her distinctive earthenwares are found on archaeological sites all over Boston.

FIGURE 25.1
Parker-Harris chamber pot heavily decorated with white clay slip that turned yellow under the vessel's lead glaze. This chamber pot was found at the nearby Three Cranes Tavern site.

The Parker-Harris pottery was made in several distinct types: one a deep-black glaze with arches of yellow slip decorations, and another with red and green blotches and similar arches. The example shown in the main photo is the red and green type with a simple band of slip and a star or sun motif (figure 25.2). Redwares, including this mug, are often looked at with indifference by archaeologists because the ceramic type is extremely common on sites and often undecorated, making analysis difficult. In Charlestown, however, the redwares produced by the local potters come in a fantastic array of forms, decorations, and colors, which allows archaeologists today to reexamine this important industry, make associations between potters and the appearances of the vessels they produced, and generally unlock data from these common artifacts that it is often difficult or impossible to obtain elsewhere.

FIGURE 25.2
Detail of clay slip decoration on the Parker-Harris mug.

Redwares like this mug were some of the least expensive ceramics available on the market. As discussed in artifact 23, because of the expensive porcelains found in the tavern's privies, the Three Cranes Tavern was presumably an establishment that catered to a high-end clientele; nevertheless, these mugs were extremely common in the artifacts recovered. It is likely that the Long family that owned the tavern bought inexpensive mugs, favoring the more decorated kinds, because they would frequently break, and the owners did not want to be constantly replacing expensive imported mugs when cheap alternatives were available from the potter's store next door.

At the time this mug was purchased, the Three Cranes was also owned by a woman, Mary Long. Not only was it rare for a woman to own her own business in mid-eighteenth-century Boston, but it was even rarer for that woman to be neighbors with another woman who *also* owned her own business. Together, these two women were heads of two of the most important businesses in Charlestown, making them both prominent and powerful businesspeople in colonial Charlestown.

26. Bottle Seal

1730–1760 | John Carnes Site, North End

From October to December 1992, ten archaeologists from John Milner Associates, a private archaeology firm, excavated 1,900 square feet of intact archaeological deposits from the former Paddy's Alley on what was expected to be a seventeenth-century house of the Paddy family (figure 26.1). At the time of the dig, the site was located in a parking lot under the expressway (Route 93) that was about to be converted into a tunnel as part of the Big Dig project. The archaeologists recovered tens of thousands of artifacts from an intact archaeological site, but not those of the Paddy family, as they were expecting. The archaeologists found numerous eighteenth-century deposits and features that they hypothesized were associated with John Carnes; their previous research indicated that he had owned the property. This was confirmed when they found multiple custom wine bottle labels, or seals, with John Carnes's name clearly marked on them.

John Carnes was born in Boston in 1698. His first wife passed away in 1720, and John married Sarah Baker two years later. Sarah and John produced fourteen children. In 1729, John and his large family moved to Paddy's Alley, which had a stone house, four tenements or apartments, and two wells.[1] At some point in his early life, John trained as a pewterer, likely as an apprentice under a master pewterer.

By the time he purchased the Paddy's Alley property, his pewter-turning

FIGURE 26.1
Photo of excavations in progress at the John Carnes/Paddy's Alley site (photo courtesy of John Milner Associates, Inc.).

business was in full swing. Interestingly, Carnes was not the lone craftsperson in the neighborhood. His direct neighbors included a shoemaker, a carpenter, a barber, a wig maker, and a tailor.[2]

FIGURE 26.2
Eighteenth-century
wine bottle with
preserved cork.
Custom glass bottle
seals were placed
on the bodies of
bottles like this
to identify their
owners.

Sarah, John's second wife, died in 1740, and John married for a third time, wedding Dorothy Farnum. Although John and Dorothy did not produce additional children, Dorothy did raise John's enormous family. John was an incredibly wealthy individual; because he produced goods in high demand and quality, he was able to use his products to leverage goods and services. He was even able to trade sugar and sets of pewter utensils for an education for his son John at Harvard University.[3]

John senior died in 1760 as one of the wealthiest men in New England. His estate included nearly 700 pounds of pewter molds, which is more than twice the amount of all other contemporary pewterers documented at that time, combined. His ability to have custom-made wine bottles (see figure 26.2 for a noncustomized eighteenth-century bottle) is one of the clearest signs of this wealth.

John's pewter goods are exceedingly rare, but are recognized as some of the finest pewter work done in Boston's history. Before anyone gets defensive about Paul Revere, Revere worked in much more valuable metals, not pewter. Two examples of Carnes's pewter survive. One is an ornate lidded mug with a distinct "Carnes Boston" mark, currently in the collection of the Winterthur Museum in Delaware. The second, now in private possession, was found at a thrift store.

In the seventeenth century, Boston relied heavily on importation of most goods, because its domestic economy was based on the maritime and fishing industries. The eighteenth century saw a radical transformation in this system. With the stability of the colonies and the ever-increasing numbers of craftspeople immigrating to Boston, bringing their knowledge, and building the necessary infrastructure, Boston and the surrounding area began to become self-sufficient on numerous fronts. While the docks and shoreline remained important throughout the history of Boston, the focus on industry began to spread inward from the coast, expanding the wealth and economy of Boston from its shoreline into what is today its downtown areas.

Paddy's Alley was located in an area that would have been part of the North End before the construction of the raised highway that destroyed a significant portion of the neighborhood and permanently "detached" the rest of the North End from the main part of the city. On today's map, the site is essentially located in the Greenway park between the Bostonian Hotel and the Tunnel Administration building.

Looking at historic photos of the area, one finds it truly remarkable that this archaeological site survived at all. In the nineteenth century, already one hundred years after John Carnes left, the area was dominated by densely packed brick structures with minimal distance between them. It is only in the areas where the building foundations did not dig through the archaeology that the site actually survived.

27. Soldering Iron

1730–1760 | John Carnes Site, North End

Pewter is an ancient material that even turns up in Egyptian graves as far back as 1450 B C.[1] The soft, silvery metal is mostly tin with added elements, including lead, antimony, and other soft metals. Overall, it is a relatively inexpensive material with a low melting point that allowed craftspeople to create dishes, cups, and other wares for use in the home and elsewhere (figure 27.1).

The pewter industry flourished in the eighteenth century, with Boston at its center because of the concentration of local pewterers producing high-quality goods.[2] The eventual decline in the use of pewter happened in the late 1700s, when cheaply made English ceramics flooded the market, replacing the equally inexpensive pewter goods with whiter-colored wares and their sometimes colorful decorations.

Before it fell out of favor, pewter was present in the most popular ware of its time. It accounted for most of the dishes and vessels used at homes throughout Boston. Numerous churches also relied on pewter cups and plates for communion services.[3] Probate inventories (lists of estate belongings given away at a person's death) regularly included a dozen or more pewter goods. Despite the prevalence of these items, they almost never turn up at archaeological sites.

Pewter has an incredibly low melting point—beginning at 170 degrees for some types. This temperature was easily achieved at home with a modest flame. Because of this trait, damaged pewter items could easily be melted down or repaired with basic tools. In addition, because it was such a relatively inexpensive material with almost unlimited recycling potential, broken or damaged vessels could be brought back to the pewterer and melted down in exchange for new items or easily repaired at little cost. Even after house fires, the melted pewter remaining in ruins could be scavenged and recycled.

This is a far cry from ceramics, which when broken were nearly impossible to repair without serious negative consequences for usability. For this reason, broken ceramics turn up by the thousands at many historic sites, but nobody would ever bother to discard a piece of pewter. This "missing" artifact in the archaeological record is a challenge for archaeologists; we often have to interpret the use of various types of dinnerware without finding the type that would have been the most commonly present on a table. Pewter is not the only "missing" artifact. Wooden plates and leather mugs were also common objects at the dinner table, especially in lower- and middle-income households. These objects typically do not survive in the ground.

FIGURE 27.1
Pewter mug with a turned body and cast handle, which would have been soldered together using tools similar to the one shown in the main image (Aberdeen 1936 [ca.]; photo courtesy of the National Gallery of Art).

FIGURE 27.2

Eighteenth-century
etching of a pewter
workshop showing
wheel-turning,
soldering, and
other techniques
represented by tools
recovered at the
John Carnes pewter
workshop (Diderot
1771).

Even though over 60,000 artifacts were found at the John Carnes archaeological site, almost no actual fragments of pewter were recovered. Nevertheless, numerous pieces of pewter-working equipment (figure 27.2) and
tools were found, including this soldering iron. Similar to the kiln furniture
found at the Parker-Harris pottery site in Charlestown and nearly all Native
stone-tool production sites found in Boston, artifacts used in the production
of goods, and waste products from the production, are often more common
than examples of the finished goods. This soldering iron would have been
used to fuse together various casts and turned pewter elements.

Irons would have been attached to a wooden handle and then placed into
a fire to heat. Because not much heat is needed to melt pewter, pewter making was easier to do in the densely populated neighborhood that this area
of the North End used to be. Other tools recovered from the site include
files used for finishing pewter edges, gouges used to form pewter disks on
turning wheels, and various cast-metal elements. As a symbol of a once-great
industry in Boston, this tiny iron object illustrates the work of one of the
city's greatest craftsmen.

28. Teapot

1762–1775 | Three Cranes Tavern, Charlestown

Creamware was the grand marshal in a parade of inexpensive English ceramics that transformed the American dining table at the end of the eighteenth century. In the 1750s, Josiah Wedgewood mastered production of an inexpensive cream-colored ceramic, and he began exporting the ware to the American colonies in 1762.[1] The thin and light butter-yellow plates with a refined style were unlike their stark gray-white predecessors of the more expensive white salt-glaze stoneware and a far cry from the relatively chunky style and boldly decorated tin glazes (artifact 15) they replaced. The popularity of this ceramic, helped by the purchase of a service by Queen Charlotte in 1765, was so great that it led to the downfall of the easily replaceable and repairable pewter goods made right in Boston by merchants like John Carnes (artifact 27), despite the greater fragility of the product and the added expense of shipping it overseas.

This creamware teapot is a notably darker version of the ware, an indication that it is from the earliest period of manufacture, about the 1760s. This nearly intact teapot was found in privy 2 at the Three Cranes Tavern. This pot represents a *terminus post quem* (TPQ; that is, "limit after which") of 1762 for the privy. TPQs are used by archaeologists to define the earliest a deposit could occur, based on the invention or production date of the youngest object in the deposit. In other words, there is no way (without a time machine) the objects in the main deposit of privy 2 could have entered the privy until after 1762, because until that year, there was no way the teapot shown in the photo could have been present in the deposit.

Conveniently, privy 2 also has a *terminus ante quem* (TAQ), which means "limit before which." In this case, the uppermost layer of the privy contained the charred remains of the actual outhouse structure that collapsed into the privy after the fires that consumed Charlestown during the Battle of Bunker Hill on June 17, 1775. Between the TPQ and TAQ, we can state with certainty that the latest deposits in Privy 2 were added sometime between 1762 and 1775, a relatively brief time, considering the history of Boston. The one caveat is that while the items in the privy may have been *deposited* between those dates, that does not mean that everything in the privy was *made* between those dates. At home, I own an eighteenth-century antique creamware teapot. If I threw it out, that does not mean that my trash can is from the 1760s, but it does mean that the items in my trash were thrown out after 1762. Since TPQs are based on the earliest possible date, it's likely that a future archaeologist would also find in my garbage something a bit later than just eighteenth-century ceramics. It may be odd finding eighteenth- and twenty-first-century objects mixed in

FIGURE 28.1
A 1730 painting
that includes a
complete tea set
in the background
(Vanderlyn 1730).

my trash, but it would certainly tell a future archaeologist quite a bit about my personal interests.

Tea drinking as a popular Euro-American practice began after the founding of the city of Boston. Tea was brought from China to Portugal in the seventeenth century but was not drunk in England until the 1660s, when King Charles II married a Portuguese princess who was fond of the drink.[2] Royalty were trendsetters in the 1660s, 1760s, and even today, and tea, tea wares, and tea drinking exploded in popularity (figure 28.1). Many ceramic artifacts found on eighteenth-century archaeological sites in Boston are directly related to the production and drinking of tea—even children's toys.

The practice of making and consuming tea brought with it entirely new social norms and traditions that transformed the everyday lives of many early Bostonians. The presence of a new and distinct set of ceramics, coupled

with a new set of behaviors surrounding the preparation, consumption, and storage of tea, added an entirely new fashionable event to most people's days. These practices were clearly valued by Bostonians, especially the wealthy, and families throughout the colonies and England commissioned portraits and papercuts of their family in the active process of serving or consuming tea. The presence of tea on the tables of early Bostonians and the need for it to be imported would eventually become a significant factor in the American Revolution, when an entire shipment of tea was cast overboard on December 16, 1773, in protest of taxes (figure 28.2), probably only a few years after this teapot was purchased and used at the Three Cranes Tavern.

PART 4 Conflict and War
(1765–1783)

Boston played a pivotal role in the American Revolution. Brewing resentment toward the Crown began spilling over in 1765 with the passage of the Stamp Act.[1] Besides costing port cities, of which Boston was one of the largest at the time, a great deal of money when importing goods, this act fundamentally violated the law in the British constitution that did not allow taxes to be imposed on individuals without their representation in Parliament. Because the American colonists did not have representation, this costly act began to take on new significance, as the King was violating his own laws at the colonists' expense, and there was no means for the colonists to object in Parliament.

British troop presence in Boston was seen as an offense toward the colonists. On March 5, 1770, what began as a street argument between a British soldier and a wig maker's apprentice devolved into the Boston Massacre. Hostility toward the Crown finally spilled over in 1773 with the Boston Tea Party, which occurred at the docks that would have been located off Atlantic Avenue, just east of present-day Dewey Square near South Station. This act of protest destroyed an entire shipment of tea aboard several East India Company ships. In response, Parliament passed a series of acts, including the closing of Boston Harbor in 1774, until import duties could be paid on the tea that had been destroyed and the East India Company repaid for its losses. This repayment would never come.

The closing of the harbor affected all Bostonians, including loyalists and those not directly involved in trade, thereby further unifying colonists against the Crown. A boycott of British goods was declared in Philadelphia at the first Continental Congress in response to these acts, and the Crown responded to the growing unrest and unruly behavior stemming from the Boston rebellion by sending thousands of troops to the city and rescinding the colonists' power to elect representatives in the Massachusetts government. A shadow government, led by John Hancock and Samuel Adams, formed in response.

To further limit the ability of the colonists to respond violently, the newly arrived British troops were sent from their camp on Boston Common to Concord to seize ammunition and weapons. Concord residents had been warned of the impending movement of troops some days earlier, and on April 18, the infamous "Midnight Ride" revealed the exact timing of the event to villagers north and east of Boston. Approximately 700 troops departed by boat from the western shore of the Common, to begin their seventeen-mile journey to Concord. Their skirmishes there with the local militias are now known as the Battles of Lexington and Concord, and the surprising success of the colonial defense against the British troops resulted in their retreat to Boston. As word of spilled blood spread through the surrounding communities, militias rushed to Boston, creating an overnight army of more than 15,000 colonists encircling the city. War had begun.

The colonial army surrounded Boston on three sides, but the lack of a navy prevented the protection of the harbor. A siege resulted, in which troops on both sides were able to amass reinforcement troops but little advancement occurred on either side. The high ground of Bunker and Breed's Hills in Charlestown and Dorchester Heights in South Boston was located in areas outside either army's territory, but the hills' prominent height and location were known by both sides to possess key strategic value in defending or attacking the city.

In May 1775, British receipt of over 6,000 additional troops led to a decision to attempt the capture and fortification by the British of high ground in both places on June 18. The colonists, having been tipped off, decided to secretly take and fortify Breed's Hill in Charlestown on the night of June 15. Their plan went unnoticed by the British that night, but the next morning, British troops saw the fortifications and attacked Charlestown in what would be called the Battle of Bunker Hill.

In July and August 1775, General George Washington, who had recently taken command of the Continental Army, conducted several skirmishes at the boundaries between the two armies in Roxbury and Charlestown with little success. By winter, the army was suffering from a lack of gunpowder, the British were suffering from a lack of wood, and both were suffering from disease and discontent over the ongoing siege. On December 5, Colonel Henry Knox led the transportation of sixty tons of cannons captured at Fort Ticonderoga in New York State to Boston in support of Washington's army. Months later, Washington devised a night fortification of the Dorchester Heights hill, much like the earlier fortification of Breed's Hill. On the night of March 5, a team of several thousand troops and several cannons that had recently arrived marched down Boston Street in Dorchester, through what would become Andrew Square, and up the hill in South Boston to fortify Dorchester Heights.

At sunrise, the British saw once again that high ground had been taken by American troops in the night. From their vantage point, the Americans were able to view and fire upon British troops, camps, and ships in Boston and the harbor, and the distance and height commanded by the colonists made defensive volleys from the British position ineffective. Realizing their defeat, the British began the long task of evacuating Boston. Under an agreement that they not be fired on, British troops boarded over one hundred ships and, after several days awaiting fair weather, evacuated on March 17, 1776, thus ending the active military engagement of Boston proper, but ensuring that the harbor and Boston's leaders would play a pivotal role in the ongoing efforts toward American independence.

29. Gunflint

1775 | Boston Common, Downtown

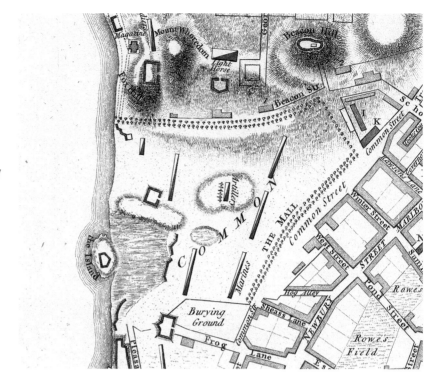

Imagine you are a British soldier stationed on Boston Common. It's a warm May day in 1775, and war is brewing. Following a long sea journey, your regiment has recently arrived to protect the Crown's interests in Boston Harbor and to quell the rebellious colonists. You have been stationed on the Common, the town's cow pasture, where you are surrounded on three sides by colonists (figure 29.1). Your commanding officers are stationed in the massive John Hancock mansion overlooking the Common from Beacon Hill, while you are essentially camping in a tent for a good part of the ten-month siege of Boston. What do you leave behind?

So much of Boston's Revolutionary War narrative focuses on the movement and actions of people across the landscape of Boston and the rest of eastern Massachusetts. On Boston Common, we have the opportunity to see these camps where troops were stationed between the actions that are so celebrated by historians. Archaeological surveys were conducted on the Common in the 1980s and early 1990s, resulting in a sample of the entire Common. This archaeology is made somewhat difficult by the actions of the Olmstead brothers in 1910. Although they are rightly celebrated for their contributions to the Common, its landscape, and the overall health of its plants, their major project on the Common was to dig up and restore the majority of the soil in the park, essentially jumbling many of the archaeological resources of the undeveloped park in the process. However, in one area in particular, near the Boylston MBTA station, archaeological evidence for these camps remained clear and preserved.

Archaeologists recovered six gunflints, one of which is shown in the main photo, three musket balls (figure 29.2), and other weapon-related artifacts. These artifacts are certainly not unique; there are plenty of revolutionary-era guns with intact flints, and many lead balls have been collected, excavated, and looted from revolutionary sites around the country. Gunflints were carefully shaped pieces of stone that were clamped onto rifles using a hammer screw. When the gun was cocked, the gunflint was held in a spring-loaded hammer, so that when the trigger of the rifle was pulled, the gunflint would strike a flat piece of metal called a *frizzen*, which caused a spark that would light the gunpowder in the barrel and propel the musket ball out of the rifle.

The Common would have been home for these troops. They would have eaten meals, paraded, slept, used the bathroom, and passed the time, all within the bounds of the Common. Without doubt, these activities would have left numerous fragments of artifacts scattered across the Common. Historic records state that the troops dug holes in the Common and built rough structures as privies or outhouses. Perhaps there are still undiscovered concentrations of artifacts from these troops. The Olmstead renovations have clearly left their mark on the Common's archaeology, but sites like the Revolutionary War camp on the Common demonstrate just how small an area needed to be left intact to document significant events in Boston's history.

30. Bar Shot

June 17, 1775 | City Square, Charlestown

The Battles of Lexington and Concord, the first attack of the American Revolution, invigorated colonial troops, which successfully pushed back British Regulars to Boston. The resulting siege of Boston was a two-sided process. British troops kept pressure on the economy and people of Boston through their constant presence and surveillance in the city and Boston Harbor, and colonial troops kept the British from leaving the city by fortifying the necks and rivers surrounding Boston.[1]

This activity came to a head the night of June 16, 1775. Tipped off that British troops were planning on taking high ground in Boston and Charlestown, Colonel William Prescott and a group of 1,200 colonists secretly took Breed's Hill, which overlooked the towns of Charlestown and Boston.[2] Under the cover of darkness, the troops dug a roughly rectangular trench at the crest of the hill and fortified it and other areas of Charlestown.

The next morning, British troops were shocked to see the fortifications atop Breed's Hill. The captain of the HMS *Lively*, a British man-of-war ship located off the coast of Charlestown, upon seeing the fortifications on the crest of Breed's Hill, immediately began firing on the fort.[3]

A brief cease-fire was followed by new volleys of destruction from the six British guns and howitzers placed on Copp's Hill in the North End and from the other British ships in the harbor; all the while the colonists continued building and improving the fortifications on Breed's Hill, cheering mockingly as cannonballs landed nearby[4] (figure 30.1).

By noon on June 17, under blue skies and full sun, the British landed near the eastern corner of Charlestown and began amassing troops in preparation for a march on Breed's Hill. The first attack on the fortification occurred at 3:00 p.m. and was met with strong resistance by the colonists, resulting in a retreat by the Regulars. During the second attack, the city of Charlestown was set ablaze (artifact 31).

The guns from Copp's Hill, along with artillery fired from the *Somerset* in

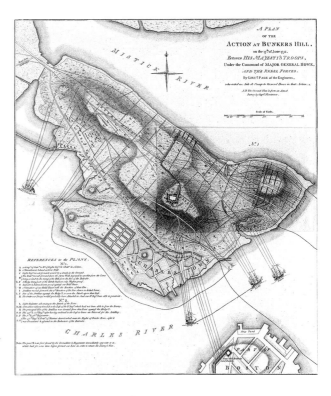

FIGURE 30.1
Map depicting ships in Boston Harbor firing upon Charlestown and fortifications on Breed's Hill, site of the future Bunker Hill Monument (Page 1793, courtesy of the Leventhal Map Center at the Boston Public Library).

the harbor, turned toward the mostly abandoned town in a deliberate attempt to erase Charlestown from the map.[5] Three-inch-wide and four-pound cast-iron cannonballs, including the one shown in the main photo and figure 30.2, were fired at the wooden homes and businesses of Charlestown residents, and the heat of the cannonballs and incendiary shot resulted in a blaze that quickly spread throughout the entire town, consuming all standing structures. Bar shot is two individual cannonballs connected by an iron bar, which would spin when fired and cause damage to sails, as well as to the homes of Charlestown. The Battle of Bunker Hill endured two more British advances, in front of a curtain of thick black smoke rising from the lost city and lit from above by a cloudless sunny sky.

By evening, the colonists had retreated past Bunker Hill to Charlestown, and the British troops had captured the Charlestown peninsula. Although it was an overall loss, the fortification and defense of Breed's Hill demonstrated the strength and organization of the seemingly disorganized and inexperienced rebel forces, perhaps to the surprise of both sides in the conflict.

31. Charcoal

FIGURE 31.1
Charlestown burning, June 17, 1775 (unknown artist, 1783).

On the eve of the American Revolution, Charlestown was a bustling town enjoying economic success brought about by its successful exports, such as pottery, rum, and ships. Under the constant threat of British attack in the early part of 1775, the residents of Charlestown began retreating from the city, taking with them their valuables and their trades. The potters, for instance, joined their relatives and colleagues in surrounding towns.

That summer, Charlestown contained about 400 houses[1] centered on what is today City Square, where the Three Cranes Tavern was located. By the time fires consumed Charlestown, all but a few homes had been completely abandoned; the destruction of the town thus resulted in a great loss of structures but not a great loss of life.

The charcoal fragments seen in the main photograph are portions of the floor of the Three Cranes Tavern, which burned on June 17, 1775 (figure 31.1). These and other fragments of charcoal found within the upper levels of the archaeological site are all that remain of the wooden building that played such a significant role in the daily lives of Charlestown residents and visitors.

The townspeople who chose to return to Charlestown found a city in complete ruin. Insurance values for the lost buildings were set at £500,000. Around 1776 the City Square area was cleared, and vast quantities of soil and surrounding artifacts were pushed into the gaping hole to fill the space that had once supported the great tavern.[2]

In 1788, the townspeople of Charlestown met and voted that the land on which the Three Cranes Tavern once stood would never again be developed, both to leave a memorial to what the town had lost and also to create an open market square for trade.[3]

Slowly, the lots in the square were sold or granted to the town of Charlestown; by the end of the nineteenth century, the property was entirely public land without standing buildings.[4] The open space received a monumental fountain and circular park in the mid-nineteenth century, creating a circular rotary around City Square. Around the turn of the twentieth century, the Boston Elevated Street Railway, a railroad on stilts, was installed across the eastern half of the square, and the western portion was converted into a small park and parking lot with a tiny obelisk-shaped monument to the square's history.

City Square would remain essentially undisturbed until the early 1980s, when archaeologists began testing the property in advance of the northern component of the Big Dig. The tests resulted in the discovery of what has become "Boston's Little Pompeii"—a place that burned suddenly and was left relatively untouched until uncovered by archaeologists (figure 31.2).

Excavations on the site began by running a backhoe trench through upper fills deposited on the site during 200 years of relatively passive use. When extended deeper, these trenches located not only fragments of the tavern foundation, but also a nearly intact eighteenth- and seventeenth-century landscape protected by the relative lack of development on the property and by the cap of protective fill.

In 1985, the large-scale archaeological excavations of City Square began, eventually covering thousands of square feet and producing enough seventeenth- and eighteenth-century artifacts to fill 308 standard banker's boxes. The City Square assemblage is the largest and most complete eighteenth-century assemblage recovered in Boston, and is one of the most significant eighteenth-century archaeological deposits in the country.

FIGURE 31.2
View of excavations at City Square in Charlestown (photo courtesy of the Public Archaeology Laboratory, Inc.).

32. Powder House Brick

1706–1775 | Boston Common, Downtown

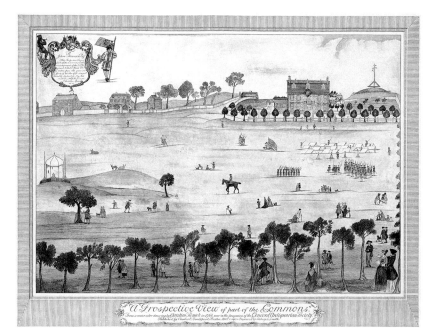

FIGURE 32.1
A 1768 view of
Boston Common
showing the powder
house on the left
(Smith 1902; image
courtesy of the
Boston Public
Library).

Since 1630, the fifty acres of Boston Common had been set aside as public pasture and later as a public park. Because of this, the Common remained relatively undeveloped, bounded to the north, east, and south by buildings and to the west by the Charles River, until land-making efforts created the Back Bay neighborhood in the nineteenth century. In the center of the park, the ancient ice sheet that once lay a mile thick on Boston left behind a distinctive hill shaped like a rising whale, with one steep side facing west and a gentle slope eastward toward downtown. Near the eastern base of the hill grew the Great Elm, a tree that predated the arrival of Europeans to Boston.

This hill and its relative great distance from buildings but close proximity to downtown created an ideal location for Boston's powder house (figure 32.1). Powder houses were structures built in most towns to store the large quantities of gunpowder a town would need to service its arms. Of course, a contained structure filled with gunpowder was a serious risk to life and limb if an accident occurred nearby. For this reason these buildings were typically placed in a relatively convenient location that was also as far away from as many things as possible, in case it exploded. The center of Boston Common was about as far from any buildings as was possible in eighteenth-century Boston.

In 1706, a multisided powder house was built on the crest of the hill in the center of the Common, giving rise to the name Powder House Hill. This name and the powder house remained in use until the arrival of the British troops

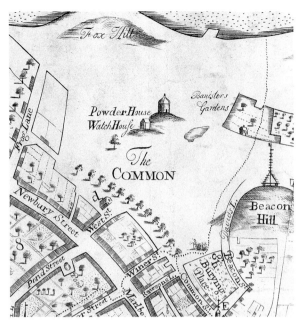

FIGURE 32.2
Map of Boston
Common showing
the powder house
(Bonner 1722;
image courtesy
of the Leventhal
Map Center at
the Boston Public
Library).

during the American Revolution; because they sought to reduce access to arms and ammunition by the rebels, the British removed the powder house and took the gunpowder.

Drawings from the period, including the famous 1722 Bonner map (figure 32.2), clearly show this powder house alongside a watch house, a type of early police station, which appears to have been located slightly downhill from the main powder house.

During the Revolution, trenches were dug all around the hilltop, which were still visible in the 1820s, when, in an effort to make the Common more park-like, they were filled. In the 1870s, the 126-foot-tall Soldiers and Sailors Monument was built on the hill to commemorate those lost in the Civil War, forever transforming its use and appearance.

During the archaeological surveys on the Common in the late 1980s, archaeologists found evidence of these filled trenches—including a spittoon from the 1830s. It is likely that local garbage was used to fill some of the deeper trenches before soil was added in order to return the hill to its natural topography.

PART 5 A Changing City in a Changing World
(1780–1983)

As Boston began to recover from the Revo-lutionary War, its industries slowly returned, allowing the city to once again grow. This time period in Boston is largely defined by two groups of people: those who had finan-cial and genealogical ties to the early settlers, the Boston Brahmins; and the newly arrived immigrants flooding into Boston.

Boston and the rest of America were growing in confidence as a new republic and were sorting out legal systems. However, some residents of Boston possessed a wealth whose foundations had been laid well be-fore the birth of the nation. This aristocracy formed a subculture and a close-knit com-munity whose members intermarried, firmly establishing their wealth and social standing through familial exclusivity.[1]

These families not only held political power in Boston and the Commonwealth, but also shaped and controlled the physical shape of Boston by buying land, removing hills, and filling in sea, swamp, and marsh to create land on which they built their homes, speculated in real estate, and created preplanned communities, which were often inhabited exclusively by those in their same socioeconomic club.[2] In the early twentieth century, the waning political and economic security of the Brahmins began to lead to a slightly more balanced power structure between the establishment and the newly arrived "other." Eventually, this "other" would become the norm in Boston.

As money moved from the once-fash-ionable waterfront and North End neigh-borhoods of Boston to the former red-light district and mudflats of the now hip and expensive Beacon Hill and Back Bay neigh-borhoods, waves of immigrants flooded in to replace them.

Although immigrants from many coun-tries were common in Boston, even in the seventeenth century, various waves are ob-servable in the town records, beginning with massive numbers of English immigrants from the 1780s to the mid-nineteenth century, Irish immigrants in the 1840s and 1850s, and finally Italian and Jewish families in the late nine-teenth and early twentieth centuries.

From 1841, when Boston began actively recording names of passengers arriving in Boston from foreign ports, to 1891, when federal records superseded state efforts, over

1,000,000 immigrants were recorded as entering the Port of Boston, an average of more than 50,000 people a year.[3]

In addition, the abolitionist movement in Boston beginning in the 1840s attracted not only members of the black community already living in Boston, but also free and escaped black people from Southern states looking to relocate in favorable surroundings.

The greatest advertisement for choosing to relocate to Boston instead of other cities and ports was the primarily positive reviews found in the handwritten letters of those who had gone to Boston and wrote home of their happiness;[4] in addition, the slightly shorter distance and lesser expense of immigrating to Boston instead of New York helped drive immigrants to the former city.

It is the dynamics between the established class and the "other" that clearly shape much of Boston's history between the Revolution and the Great Depression.

33. Massachusetts Cent

1788 | Boston Common, Downtown

This coin beautifully illustrates a period in history soon after the end of the Revolution in 1783 when the American victors were faced not only with the results of their own success—power and self-rule—but also with the responsibility to set up a new government to fill the gaps left by royal powers.

Boston's population in 1780 was just 10,000 individuals, almost 5,000 less than in 1770, before the war. The flight of the Tories, the flight from the siege, and deaths from fighting were all largely to blame for the decline in population. The first two decades after the Revolution, dramatic rises in population and economic prosperity occurred, after getting off to a slow start; there were 18,000 residents in 1790 and 25,000 by 1800.[1]

Several important things occurred after the war in Boston, beginning in the 1780s: the Massachusetts constitution was passed, which declared that "all Men are born free and equal." This assertion resulted in a lawsuit by the enslaved Elizabeth Freeman (Mum Bett) and the eventual abolishment of slavery in Massachusetts; a lack of demand caused Boston's shipbuilding industry to crash; Boston established its own direct trade with China, resulting in a resurgence of trade in the city; and tremendous numbers of English immigrants began to fill areas such as the North End. Throughout this period, Boston confirmed its place at the political and emotional center of the new nation.[2]

In 1787, the Constitutional Convention was held in Philadelphia to draft a constitution that would settle disputes that had arisen between states after the Revolution by establishing a strong federal government.

FIGURE 33.1
Obverse of 1788
Massachusetts cent.

Without a national mint and given the abandonment of the British pound, several states began producing their own coinage. Massachusetts first started producing copper coins in the value of a half-penny and one cent in 1787. The dies were produced by Joseph Callender, an apprentice of Paul Revere, who had a shop on State Street,[3] and about 100,000 coins were struck. This coin was struck the following year (obverse shown in figure 33.1), the same year the United States voted in its first president, George Washington.

It was Thomas Jefferson who came up with the idea of establishing the dollar based on the Spanish silver dollar, with subdivisions including the cent ($^1/_{100}$ of a dollar), dime ($^1/_{10}$ of a dollar), and so on.[4] A federal resolution in 1785 established Jefferson's ideas as policy, but the local mints throughout the new country used several systems that typically included a percentage copper weight to a troy ounce of silver. Massachusetts was the only mint—at

FIGURE 33.2
View of the
Massachusetts
State House built
in 1795 (Curtis
and Cameron
1808–1812 [ca.];
image courtesy of
the Boston Public
Library).

the time including state and private operations—to use the decimal system, establishing the cent as $1/100$ of a dollar.

The confusion of coinage systems, which often resulted in the use of foreign coins for commerce, led in 1792 to the creation of the US Mint, which began creating and circulating the only legal coinage.

The 1788 coin depicts a Massachusett Native American holding a bow and arrow, and features a star above his shoulder. This symbol would later become the Great Seal of the Commonwealth of Massachusetts, reflecting the commonwealth's Native heritage as well as establishing the state's self-identity (figure 33.2), which persisted throughout the eighteenth century and on into the present.

34. Sail Needle

Eighteenth Century | City Square, Charlestown

The maritime industry was the heart of Boston's economy from its foundation through the nineteenth century. Although Boston was home to numerous tradesmen and -women (artifacts 24 and 27), the vast majority of workers were tied to the maritime trades either directly through shipbuilding and sailing, or through the sale and trade of the goods that arrived daily at Boston's Town Dock at Faneuil Hall and other trading points such as Long Wharf (figure 34.1). Shipbuilding at the turn of the nineteenth century was focused on the shores of Charlestown and East Boston, wood being brought from inland to form the vessels and numerous structures and industries centered at the shore for the building and installation of related goods such as ropewalks (for the manufacture of rope), chain forges, and sail shops.

The artifact shown in the main photo is a flat copper sail needle used for maintaining sails on the tall ships that once filled Boston Harbor. After the Revolutionary War, Britain remained a powerhouse at sea after defeating the French during the Napoleonic wars. The United States, still flush with its victory over Britain, was frequently embarrassed and abused by the British navy, and Boston sailors were regularly kidnapped and "impressed," or forced, into the Royal Navy. Britain also restricted trade between the United States and France. The result was the declaration by President Jefferson of a self-imposed embargo in 1807[1] on trade between the United States and Britain, which caused a major depression in the New England economy (with Boston at its heart). Ships sat becalmed in Boston's great harbor (figure 34.2).

FIGURE 34.1
Revere etching of Boston Harbor with Long Wharf in the center (Revere 1768; image courtesy of the Boston Public Library).

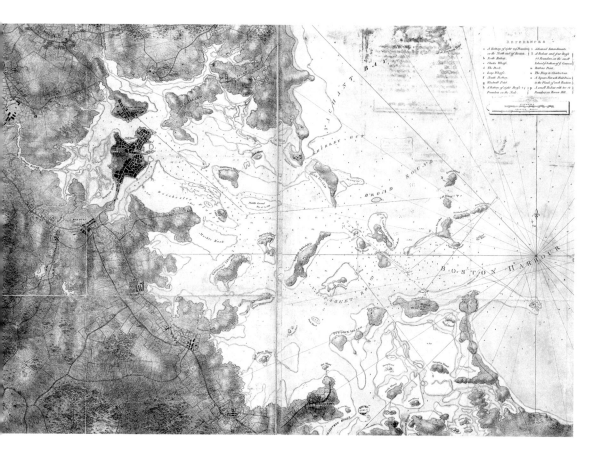

FIGURE 34.2
Map of Boston
Harbor in 1775
(Des Barres 1775;
photo courtesy of
the Norman B.
Leventhal Map
Center at the
Boston Public
Library).

The oppression and harassment of American sailors by the British, rising hostilities between the British-supported Native peoples in the West, and Canadian resistance to American expansion northward brought about a declaration by Congress of war against Britain in 1812.[2]

The major ports in the Northeast immediately opposed the War of 1812, as they correctly predicted that the powerful British navy would react with blockades.[3] Without the support of New York and the other northeastern states, including Massachusetts, America waged war on Britain in Canada, at America's western borders, and at sea.

The self-imposed embargo and the British blockade were disastrous to Boston's economy, leading to massive unemployment among men employed in its maritime industry. Despite Boston merchants' widespread evasion of the British blockade and the embargo laws, the economic effects across the young United States created widespread anger. Southern and northern states whose economies were dependent on the export of certain goods (cotton in the South and ships in the North, for example) were devastated by their inability to export goods to Britain and other nations and to import other critical goods from each other.

Resentment toward the unpopular war led to growing support of the British on the part of many New England merchants and nearly caused New England to secede from the United States. At the end of 1814, New England leaders met in Hartford, Connecticut, to draw up a list of demands to be presented to President Madison, such as that trade embargos be limited to sixty days and that a two-thirds majority be required in Congress to declare war.[4] Representatives of the Hartford Convention from Massachusetts were sent to Washington, DC, to present the demands, but before they arrived, a major victory by America at the Battle of New Orleans and the resultant peace treaty caused embarrassment for the New England states, whose actions appeared to deny support to their country during a war.

The outcome of the War of 1812 was a bit of a stalemate between the United States and Britain. Neither country lost territory, so the long-term effects of the war on relations between the two countries were negligible. In Boston, one long-term impact of the war was the shift in Bostonians' reliance on goods that were made locally. As a major port town, Boston had been able to rely on goods from abroad such as textiles for many of its major needs, but with the outbreak of the war, the local economy looked inward for its supplies of raw goods, focusing on the construction of new mills along major rivers. The Lowell mill system and the Blackstone Canal, both built in the 1820s, have direct ties to the industrial growth that arose because of the War of 1812.

35. Tortoiseshell Comb

Nineteenth Century | Boston Common, Downtown

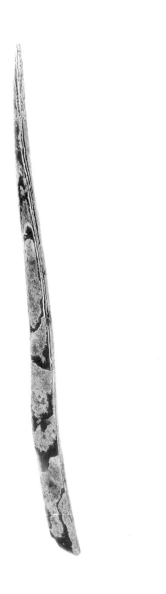

Women played a major role in the War of 1812, as they did during the American Revolution—from maintaining homes and families during war to nursing the injured and sick left on the battlefield, sewing and repairing military uniforms, and even spying. In major forts such as Fort Independence, which is known by most Bostonians as Castle Island (figure 35.1), American officers stationed within the walls of the captured British fort during the War of 1812 often were accompanied by their wives.

Officers' wives held positions of influence and power among women in Boston society (figure 35.2). Besides being some of the only women allowed to live at the fort, many of these women desired to maintain the same daily activities they were accustomed to in their stately homes in and around the city. These could include parties, teas, and various other events attended by both the ladies resident at the fort and others who would travel to the fort specifically for these events.[1]

In addition to creating a different atmosphere within the male-dominated landscape of the fort, such events allowed for the continuance of social and political connections between these women. The situation of many women in positions of power had been drastically altered by their relocation to forts. No longer were they living on their large estates in Roxbury or Dorchester or in their row homes in the North End. Now they were far from most friends and

FIGURE 35.1
A 1925 view of
Castle Island and
Fort Independence
in South Boston
(Fairchild Aerial
Surveys, Inc., 1925;
photo courtesy of
the Boston Public
Library).

FIGURE 35.2
An 1818 painting
of a wealthy woman
(Sully 1818).

family and subject to a military system that showed little concern for their comfort, their disrupted lives, or their social interactions, as war spread through the colony.

Archaeological investigations at Fort Independence in the 1970s ahead of the bicentennial celebrations revealed a massive privy (outhouse) in the middle of the open parade ground inside the fort.[2] The vast majority of the assemblage recovered from the privy comprised whole plates, platters, and other household goods that were tossed into the privy, apparently in haste. It appears that when the order was given to abandon the fort, the military occupants, rather than take these goods with them, decided to toss the entirety of their household ceramics into the privy, even though these were in perfectly usable condition. This may have been because the owners feared that these objects would fall into enemy hands if kept, or perhaps because they simply had no use for them when they left the fort.

Among the artifacts recovered were several personal items that belonged to the women who lived in the fort. These included a tortoiseshell comb (figure 35.3) like the one in the main photo and a silk slipper. These refined objects were the height of fashion and frivolity in the late eighteenth century and represent deliberate and visible attempts by these women to assert their wealth, social position, and femininity in their masculine environment.

FIGURE 35.3
Tortoiseshell comb. Note the teeth, which are similar to the archaeological example shown in the main photo (Creative-museum 2010; image courtesy of Wikimedia Commons).

36. Shell-Edge Pearlware

1819–1830 | African Meeting House, Beacon Hill

The African Meeting House was built in 1806 on the north side of Beacon Hill[1] (figure 36.1). In the early nineteenth century, this region was home to a sizable group within Boston's black community. Most of these individuals and families were born free, but some were escapees from the South, and others were freed during their lifetimes.

The structure that was built served many purposes for the community: it was a Baptist church, a meeting place for events, and a cultural center for the community, and the basement of the building contained two apartments.

Archaeological investigations behind the African Meeting House have revealed incredible volumes of data on the lifeways of these people, poorly represented in historic records[2] (figure 36.2).

One central figure in the story of this building is Domingo Williams, a black man who lived with his family and two other free black men in one of the apartments under the African Meeting House between 1819 and 1830.[3]

Domingo was a caterer—and not just any caterer, but *the* caterer to both the black community and many others in Boston. He was responsible for providing not only food for events, but also the dishes on which to serve the food; entertainment; decorations; and linens. He generally served the local community as the go-to party planner. It appears that he ran his catering business from his home, because many of the thousands of fragments of ceramics recovered behind the Meeting House were from the same set of dishes. Archaeologists have interpreted this set of nearly matching dishes to be those used by Domingo in his successful catering business and also used for community events at the African Meeting House.[4] It is clear that Domingo took great pride in his business, regularly replacing broken dishes with identical or near-identical pieces, a practice resulting in the great numbers of similar-looking dishes found at the site. At this time, only the wealthiest Boston households would have been willing or able to maintain a matching set of dishware, because of the necessity of constantly replacing broken pieces and a general inability to purchase large quantities of identical dishware at the same time; these factors prevented most

FIGURE 36.2
Archaeologists
excavating behind
the African
Meeting House
in 2005 (Landon
2007, cover; photo
courtesy of David
Landon).

from achieving this very visible economic achievement.

It seems that despite all the negative aspects of living in Boston during this time, the black community in Boston was still able to achieve financial success, to the point that its members were able to participate in economic markets similar to those for white Bostonians and purchase most of the same items that anyone else in Boston would have been purchasing at this time. In addition, their health may have been a bit better than the average Bostonian's, as is discussed in artifact 43.

Although Boston was the center of the abolitionist movement in the North and had banned slavery nearly thirty years prior to the construction of the church, Boston's black community nevertheless suffered discrimination and a lack of access to public and private resources.

Despite this fact, the most incredible aspect of the African Meeting House artifact assemblage is that if you did not know that the artifacts recovered from the site were associated with a black community that had relatively lower income than most of residents of Boston, you would never be able to tell from the artifacts themselves, because they resemble most other nonblack sites in Boston at this time.

37. Cowbell

1770–1830 | Boston Common, Downtown

Boston Common is Boston's "backyard," with about fifty acres of open park-land, trees, and paved paths, and just enough hills to make it interesting to look at, too. While it is considered by most to be the oldest park in the country—it was specifically set aside for public use in 1634—it was not formally made a park until 1830.

In the 1630s, Boston was by no means an urban metropolis, and most Bostonians relied at least in part on home gardens. Many early Bostonians had berry patches and crops growing behind their "downtown" house lots, and large gardens can be seen in the early 1722 Bonner map of the city of Boston. The Common itself was part of the 1625–1630 garden plot that William Blaxton created for himself beside his home on the western hill edge of the Shawmut peninsula that would later become Boston.

The primary purpose of the Common in 1634 was to house the cows of Boston residents in an easily observable area where the cattle could eat grass and have access to fresh water at the Frog Pond spring or the various vernal pools that appeared in low areas on the Common during heavy rainfall (figures 37.1 and 37.2). Each resident of Boston (that is, each free adult white male) was able to purchase a share of the Common, which would allow him to house his cattle and sheep there.

FIGURE 37.1 Etching of cows on Boston Common under the Great Elm (unknown artis,t 1815; courtesy of the Boston Public Library).

Eventually, the Common's turf could not handle the heavy trotting and grazing by unregulated cow herds. In reaction, a cap of seventy cows was placed on the Common in 1643. One cow was allowed per person (though four sheep could be substituted for each cow, if desired), and no horses.[1] An exception to the "no horses" rule was granted to Thomas Oliver, an elder of the First Church, who was apparently quite popular and therefore allowed to keep one horse on the Common.

The pastoral views of the Common changed radically in the 1770s, as British troop arrivals on a grand scale altered the landscape from pasture to military camp. Thousands of troops were housed in tents on the Common, and they proceeded to dig trenches and create earthworks to defend the camp and observe the activities of the rebels.

As the scars of trenches slowly eroded and were covered by grass,

FIGURE 37.2
Cows on the
Common (Curtis
and Cameron
1808–1812 [ca.];
image courtesy
of the Boston
Public Library).

the people of Boston looked on their Common with new eyes. In 1830, when cows were formally banned from the Common forever, it was transformed from pasture to park.[2]

This cowbell was found on the Common during the archaeological survey carried out in preparation for the installation of new lighting in 1987. Its color comes from the iron conservation treatment that was used to stop rust and further deterioration. Because cows were banned in 1830, we can date the bell to sometime between 1634 and 1830, although it probably dates to the end of the eighteenth century or early nineteenth century.

Like Boston as a city, the use and purpose of Common for the residents who lived nearby were constantly changing. The open space, central location, and contrast with the surrounding urban environment made the Common a centerpiece of Bostonians' daily life and the city's history, for events ranging from hangings to parades to political gatherings.

38. Nib

1841–1847 | Brook Farm, West Roxbury

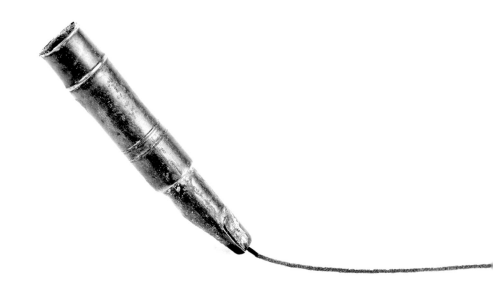

In the nineteenth century, Boston was a leader in the transcendentalist movement, which celebrated nature, independence, and intellectual endeavor. The city during this period was a soup-to-nuts publishing mecca where authors could work within a community that appreciated verse and knowledge. The Old Corner Bookstore, built in 1712, was the site of the publishing giant Ticknor and Fields, which opened in the building in 1836.[1] In the nineteenth century, the company produced books for Charles Dickens, Henry Wadsworth Longfellow, Harriet Beecher Stowe, and Mark Twain, among others, not only solidifying Boston's reputation as a literary hub, but also establishing America as a seedbed for great writers.

FIGURE 38.1
Nathaniel
Hawthorne
(Andrew 1850 [ca.];
image courtesy of
the Boston Public
Library).

Boston not only published great authors, but produced them as well. Harvard College (now Harvard University) educated Ralph Waldo Emerson and Henry David Thoreau; and writers including Nathaniel Hawthorne (figure 38.1), Louisa May Alcott, and Margaret Fuller all called Boston home during significant periods of their lives.

In 1841, a group of scholars in the transcendentalist movement formed a utopian community in the southwest corner of Boston. Following the principles of transcendentalism, these ambitious individuals created a farm where money and food were apportioned equally across genders, in the hope that sharing labor would allow for greater leisure and academic exploration, including writing. This became the most celebrated utopian experiment in the United States.[2]

Brook Farm (figure 38.2), as it became known, attracted many writers, including Henry David Thoreau, Bronson Alcott, and Nathaniel Hawthorne (who lived on the property for several years), and many others visited often. Hawthorne based his story *The Blithedale Romance* on a fictionalized version of his experiences in the community.[3] The book, though he claimed it was fiction, was so clearly a commentary on the realities of living in the community that reviewers (some of whom had visited or lived at the site) were able to associate specific characters and occurrences with individual members and events at Brook Farm.

Although several structures were built, the community struggled financially and lost its investors after fires claimed individual properties, including a huge,

FIGURE 38.2
An 1843 map of Roxbury showing Brook Farm (Whitney 1843; map courtesy of the Leventhal Map Center at the Boston Public Library).

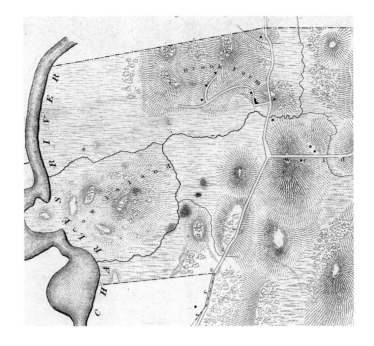

newly built experimental communal dormitory called the Phalanstery, which burned before the members were even able to use it.[4] The lack of insurance on their buildings and the loss of financial backing resulted in the farm's closing just months later.

While the community was short-lived, archaeological investigations on Brook Farm in the early 1990s produced mountains of artifacts and historical data on the occupants, including the quill nib shown in the main photo. While it is not possible to associate the artifact with any one author in particular, it is possible that one of the literary giants who lived on or visited the property penned a letter or page of their manuscript using the quill nib while at the property.

The ink masters (stoneware bottles that contained reserves of black ink) and ink bottles, which would be refilled from the ink masters, both found in abundance on the site, attest to the residents' focus on literary pursuits. Stone slates and slate pencils were also recovered in profusion. These were associated with the school located on the property, where boys and girls were educated with the ultimate goal of preparing them for college.

Although the experimental utopian community ultimately failed, while it lasted it was a center of education, writing, and community development. Today the property is a public park and a designated National Historic and Boston Landmark.

39. New York Militia Button

1861 | Brook Farm, West Roxbury

Apart from the occasional monument, reminders of the impact of the Civil War in Boston are overshadowed by the city's role in the American Revolution. While it was for the most part physically outside the actual area of conflict, Boston gave thousands of its residents to the Union cause and was greatly affected economically by a drop in trade with the South. Unfortunately, this decline in the maritime importance of Boston during the Civil War became permanent.

Ordinary people were Boston's greatest contribution to the war. Massachusetts as a whole sent 159,165 individuals to war, of whom 12,976 did not return (figure 39.1). The Massachusetts Fifty-Fourth is the best known of Boston's Civil War contributions. This infantry regiment was composed of over 1,000 black men from across the Union and beyond—some born into slavery. Recruits began gathering at Camp Meigs in the Reedville area of Hyde Park, Boston's southernmost neighborhood, in February 1863. On May 28, 1863, the regiment left Boston under the leadership of Robert Gould Shaw, after a speech by the governor of Massachusetts. As the regiment departed, thousands of Bostonians gathered on the street to cheer and encourage this unique group of men as they headed north to Battery Wharf to board a steamship heading south to war.[1] Today, a portion of the former Camp Meigs is a state-owned park.

The far lesser-known Second Massachusetts Infantry Regiment first mustered at Camp Andrew in West Roxbury in May 1861. This camp, formed on the rear portions of the property that was formerly the Brook Farm utopian community (artifact 38), was excavated by archaeologists during their survey of Brook Farm in the early 1990s. The Massachusetts Second went on to serve in numerous important battles and events during the Civil War. In Virginia they served in the Battles of Fredericksburg and Cedar Mountain.[2]

During the excavations, archaeologists found the New York militia button seen in the main image. Robert Gould Shaw (figure 39.2) arrived at Camp Andrew in May 1861 as the second lieutenant of Company H. Shaw had recently transferred from the New York militia; in a letter written that same month, Robert asked his father to send him his militia coat because his new coat had not yet arrived and he wanted to make sure he looked the part of a soldier.[3] Although there were other New York militiamen stationed at Camp Andrew, it is possible that this button was from Shaw's overcoat.

Shaw was wounded in battle as part of the Massachusetts Second, and while healing he was offered the role of commander of the Massachusetts Fifty-Fourth infantry, the first all-black regiment in US history. He fell in battle in South Carolina in 1863, after leading his 1,100 black soldiers to glory.

FIGURE 39.2 Robert Gould Shaw (Whipple 1859–1870 [ca.]; image courtesy of the Boston Public Library).

40. Vaginal Syringe

1852–1883 | Endicott Street Privy, North End

As immigrants poured into the North End and upper-class households moved away, the neighborhood was rapidly transformed. The steady stream of merchants and sailors on the waterfront, along with a bustling urban center nearby, gave rise to a successful red-light district. This concentration of houses of prostitution centered during the nineteenth century on Ann Street, which by the end of the 1800s had such a bad reputation that the street was renamed North Street (where the Paul Revere House can be found today). In its heyday, more than half of all the brothels in Boston were located on Ann Street, which itself formed one of the boundaries of the Black Sea, Boston's red-light district, full of seedy bars and boardinghouses.[1] Just outside the Black Sea was a house of prostitution on Endicott Street, near the Hanover Street entrance to the North End.

   Mrs. Lake was the madam of the house, where she lived with her girls from 1852 to 1883. Her clients, her employees, and she herself used a privy (outhouse) just behind the building, a location typical for outhouses of all homes in Boston at the time. Although the house did not survive development in Boston, the privy in the backyard somehow escaped disturbance until archaeologists encountered it during a survey of the former Mill Pond, in advance of the Big Dig (figure 40.1). The Mill Pond was the area around today's North Station that was filled in 1828. Because of budgetary and time restrictions on the Big Dig archaeological excavations, only deposits prior to 1830 relating to the filling of Mill Pond received complete analysis. The later privy and its contents were excavated and boxed, unanalyzed. Dr. Mary Beaudry, a professor of archaeology at Boston University, along with her students, began a reanalysis of this collection in the late 2000s. Decades after the artifacts were excavated, Jade Luiz, one of Beaudry's students, discovered historic records associating the property containing the privy with a house of prostitution.[2]

   This new information offered revealing insights into the somewhat atypical artifacts found in the privy. For starters, there were a huge number of objects relating to personal hygiene. Although prostitution was illegal and its workers looked upon as unclean, the archaeological evidence from this and other similar deposits around the world shows that prostitutes greatly valued personal hygiene (as did their clients, no doubt) and maintained standards of cleanliness far exceeding those of their neighbors.[3]

FIGURE 40.2
Copaiba oil bottle
from Endicott
Street brothel's
privy.

Perhaps most notable among the artifacts recovered from the privy were thirty vaginal syringes.[4] These glass plungers are cylindrical in shape, with rounded, pierced ends that would allow for insertion and internal deployment of medicines.

These devices were used by the women of the brothel to inject various liquid douches, such as mercury, vinegar, and arsenic, as well as cleansing agents. A bottle of medicine containing copaiba oil (figure 40.2) was also found.[5] The intended remedial properties of these liquids are not clear, but many of them, including copaiba oil, a distilled tree resin oil, were capable of inducing an abortion. Cleanliness, disease prevention, and disease treatment were also likely uses for these liquids.

It is clear that both the standards of personal hygiene and the specialty medical devices found at the site were directly connected with the profession of the residents, who relied on both in reaction to and in preparation for their daily activities. The young women employed by Mrs. Lake came from nearby towns as well as foreign lands,[6] origins that would have been mirrored in their clientele of visiting merchants, sailors, and local neighborhood residents.

41. Love Token

1870–1901 | Boston Common, Downtown

FIGURE 41.1

View of the stately
architecture of
Commonwealth
Avenue in the 1870s
(Smith 1870–1879
[ca.]; courtesy of
the Boston Public
Library).

The Victorian era swept through Boston on a wave of change, as new people, land, and development drastically and permanently transformed the demographics, appearance, and size of Boston. In the middle of the nineteenth century, waves of immigrants from Europe began pouring into Boston and other East Coast cities throughout America and Canada. These immigrants were predominantly Catholics from Ireland and Italy and Jews from Eastern Europe. The new arrivals rapidly grew in number and rose to political power, upsetting the Boston Brahmin establishment of aristocratic Boston families with their ties to original settlers and old wealth.

On November 9, 1872, a massive fire swept through what are today the financial and downtown areas of Boston, destroying sixty-five acres of dense development, including homes, businesses, churches, and public buildings. Almost contemporaneous with the massive fire, the land-making efforts in the Back Bay between Boston Common and Kenmore Square resulted in the creation of more than 700 acres of land, later to be graced with stately avenues and one of Boston's first gridded street plans[1] (figure 41.1).

The influx of population, the loss of buildings, and the creation of new land brought about a fundamental restructuring of the neighborhoods of Boston. In the North End, longtime single-family homes such as the Clough House, site of an archaeological survey in 2013, were transformed into tenements for recent immigrants, and purpose-built tenements started filling vacant land or replacing larger homes. The wealthier residents of the North End began moving toward the west and south. Beacon Hill, which had only in the 1830s been transformed from the city's red-light district to its wealthiest neighborhood, suddenly had real estate competition from the massive mansions and row houses being built in newer Victorian styles on Newbury Street, Commonwealth Avenue, and Beacon Street. South Boston, which for centuries had been a relatively undeveloped cow pasture; Dorchester; and areas of Roxbury, Jamaica Plain, and Roslindale were rapidly transformed from expansive farm lots with central houses into Victorian developments. By the turn of the twentieth century, Boston was filled with three-deckers, closely spaced Victorian homes, and mansions with the highly ornamental architecture still visible throughout the city.

In downtown, two competing narratives arose from this period. On the one hand, immigrants and their children were quickly outnumbering Brahmins and growing in political power, but the Brahmins still had the advantage of land, wealth, and political connections. This influence can be seen most prominently in many drawings and descriptions of Boston written during this era

FIGURE 41.2
Etching of Victorian Bostonians on Boston Common (Homer 1858; image courtesy of the Boston Public Library).

THE BOSTON COMMON.

(whose audience was Brahmin) that were either exposés on the poor living conditions of the immigrant neighborhoods or celebrations of the elegance and Victorian splendor of the Back Bay and Beacon Hill.

Boston Common became a visual and demographic battleground. The Common was transformed from passive green space into a true park, thanks to deliberate tree plantings and the construction of wide "promenades" paralleling the Tremont, Park, and Beacon Streets edges of the park. It became highly fashionable for wealthy Bostonians, especially women, to promenade along these stately pathways dressed in their finest, to enjoy the open space of a rapidly growing city, as local children from upper-class and immigrant families played in the open spaces[2] (figure 41.2).

The artifact shown in the main photo perfectly illustrates the romantic side of the Victorian era—a love token. Love tokens were typically given to a young woman, in this case "Bertie," by a courting beau. They were almost always made from silver dimes, although this one was made from a Canadian dime. Love tokens would involve polishing one side of a dime to a smooth surface, the name or initials of the receiver then being etched on the surface. This coin's date has been polished off, but the coin depicts Queen Victoria and was minted sometime between 1870 and 1901. The piercing allowed the token to be attached to a bracelet like a charm or to a necklace. We will never know if the love token was tragically lost while Bertie promenaded in the Common or was cast from the bracelet after love soured, but it remains a tiny snapshot of one Bostonian's Victorian-era life.

42. Horse Blinder

1860–1891 | Metropolitan Horse Railroad Company Site, Roxbury

(Photo by Jennifer Poulsen; courtesy of Miles Shugar).

Boston is not well recognized for its industrial history, but its core economic resource during the nineteenth century was the manufacture of goods.[1] A subdiscipline of archaeology known as industrial archaeology has arisen relatively recently. It focuses on America's industries, their associated housing, and the infrastructure that arose around these industries. Although the Industrial Revolution is defined by the use of machinery and the replacement of individually produced hand-made goods by mass-produced goods, people were still a critical component in these new processes.

The industrial spine of Boston in the late eighteenth and early nineteenth centuries was located on the Stony Brook in Roxbury.[2] This river flowed from Hyde Park north to the Back Bay, passing through Roslindale, Jamaica Plain, and Roxbury. These areas were primarily rural in the seventeenth and early eighteenth centuries, so as manufacturing increased in Boston, attention naturally turned to less-developed rivers that would allow for the rapid construction of large-scale industrial buildings.

Businesses appeared along the course of the river, and massive factories were built abutting and covering the brook, which not only powered some of the businesses by water turbines, but also served as an open sewer and drain for the manufacturing and human waste produced therein. The river became so polluted and covered by structures that by the late 1880s, the city decided to channel it through a buried culvert. A railroad built along the buried river

FIGURE 42.I
Aerial drawing of Roxbury showing the Metropolitan Horse Railroad station in red (O. H. Bailey and Company 1888; courtesy of the Norman B. Leventhal Map Center at the Boston Public Library).

was later chosen as the location for the controversial Southwest Corridor highway project. Although the highway was never built, extensive archaeological investigations along this industrial corridor revealed extensive and significant historical data.[3] Today, the same route is now part of the MBTA's Orange Line, a state park, and a popular trail system.

In Roxbury, the Stony Brook powered the pulleys and gears of production. At the Guild and White Tannery site, archaeologists were able to find a leaching room, a boiler room, and a bark house of the leatherworking business. From 1847 to 1889, over 1,000 tons of bark a year were used to treat more than 100,000 calfskins, all powered by a steam engine.[4] Bark, typically hemlock, would be squeezed and crushed to extract naturally occurring tannic acid. This acid, the same thing that turns the water brown in black tea and in swamps, was used extensively to preserve and treat leather. Hides were first salted and then soaked in the acid mixture. Lime and arsenic were used to soften the hair on the hides, which was then scraped away. Another soaking followed before the hides were scraped a final time to reveal the processed leather.

At the neighboring Highland Foundry, large vats of molten iron were used to create household goods. The foundry was open between 1842 and 1917, and at its peak in the 1860s it was producing 3,000 stoves and over 6,000 cast-iron kitchen goods a year. Archaeologists found a cupola room where the large vats of molten iron were heated, and the charging room where the raw iron fragments were collected and sorted to be added to the furnace.[5]

FIGURE 42.2
Metropolitan Horse Railroad car passing the Winthrop House in 1857 (Unknown Artist 1857; courtesy of the Boston Public Library).

The Metropolitan Horse Railroad site, located where the Ruggles MBTA station is today on the Orange Line, was excavated as part of the Southwest Corridor archaeological dig (figure 42.1). These excavations revealed hundreds of pieces of harness leather and horse blinders like the one shown in the main photo, as well as parts used to repair the carriages. Before the advent of the electric cars used today on the MBTA, similar-looking horse-drawn versions of the vehicles were in place on numerous aboveground tracks in roads (figure 42.2). The Metropolitan Horse Railroad site revealed important data from the period when the railway was making the transition from horse-drawn cars to electric cars. Archaeologists found that even after electric train cars made horses redundant, the harness manufacturing at the rail depot continued to serve the community, which was still changing over to the new electronic technologies.[6]

43. Rock and Tar Bottle

1895 | Blake House Site, Dorchester

FIGURE 43.1
Details of Rock
and Tar medicine
bottle labels.

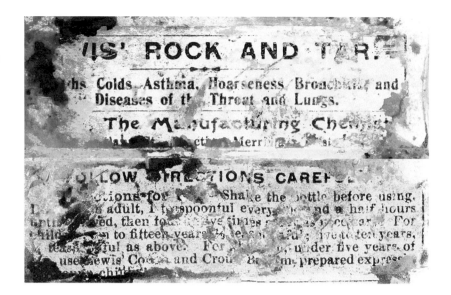

One of the most prominent developments in health care in the nineteenth century was the dramatic increase in the number of medicines available on the market, even if most of the medicines were little more than well-branded alcohol solutions and opiates. During this period, medicine came in two major categories: patent and prescription. Patent medicine included pills, liquids, or powders patented by a company that produced and sold them, but because patenting required the manufacturer to disclose the ingredients of their often dubious "medicine," manufacturers instead developed brand names and labeling that could be patented instead. This movement toward increased marketing of product design was the beginning of the modern marketing movement.

Manufacturers quickly realized the benefit of visual marketing, which caused an explosion in the advertising and marketing of goods that today has spread to food, clothing, and nearly everything else one can buy.

Prescription medicine, however, was issued by a doctor through a prescription; as is true today, both types of medicine were available at pharmacies and apothecaries. Even during this period, doctors were warning consumers of the dubious claims and potential dangers of unregulated medicine, while nevertheless issuing prescriptions for medicine with many of the same drawbacks. Unlike today, however, at that time many of the food and drug regulations did not exist, allowing claims of medical benefits to go unproven and ingredients to be sold untested.

General cleanliness was also a major issue in nineteenth-century Boston. Although smells themselves were still more associated with illness than with

FIGURE 43.2
A 1905 image of
the Lewis and
Company building
in Scollay Square.
Note the advertise-
ment for Rock and
Tar on the second
story (Boston Tran-
sit Commission
1905; photo cour-
tesy of the City of
Boston Archives).

the bacteria producing the odor, in 1701 laws were passed requiring that privies
not be constructed within forty feet of a house or well, unless they were at least
six feet in depth and did not leak their contents into the ground. The thought
was that the smell was too foul for general health, and the carts that would
often leak the privy contents across town during their nighttime emptying
were a health hazard for homeowners and neighbors. During later periods
(1810–1830), the Mill Pond that was once located between the North End
and North Station was filled in because it had become so full of carcasses,
human waste, and general garbage that it was becoming a public nuisance,
especially at low tide.[1]

Elsewhere, archaeologists working on sites associated with the end of the nineteenth century note dramatic increases in the presence of medicine bottles. At the Paul Revere site, one outhouse deposit contained 107 pharmacy bottles, 25 of which were intact.[2]

Work at the Blake House site in Dorchester revealed a massive trash deposit that was dumped in 1895 to fill in a small pond. Many of the items dumped were medicine bottles, and the wet climate of the filled-in pond preserved many of the bottle labels, allowing us to interpret what medicines were once in the bottles.[3]

The bottle shown in the main photo, Lewis' Rock and Tar (detail view in figure 43.1), was found at the Dorchester site but was manufactured in downtown Boston at the Lewis and Company wholesale druggist building on Brattle Street in the former Scollay Square, now Government Center (figure 43.2). According to the bottle, Lewis' Rock and Tar was used to treat "Cough, colds, asthma, hoarseness, bronchitis, and diseases of the throat and lungs." Perhaps for good reasons, the labels did not include a list of ingredients, nor does it appeared to have survived, although one wonders what the taste and appearance of medicine called "rock and tar" could be.

Medicine was not available equally to all. Although the black community struggled for access to high-quality health care and medicine, artifacts from the African Meeting House excavations revealed that relatively few patent medicines were being purchased, but numerous prescription medicines were procured from reputable medical institutions, as a conscious and deliberate choice, although medical expertise was generally exclusively reserved for the white community. In addition, intestinal parasite eggs (e.g., roundworm and whipworm), which can be found in every Boston privy (artifact 12), were relatively fewer in number at the African Meeting House than in all other comparable privies of the period. The overall impact of these three findings at the African Meeting House is to suggest that through deliberate resistance to the exclusivity of the medical system, the individuals who lived in the apartments under the African Meeting House may have preserved relatively good health by comparison with that in white households, despite ingrained social obstacles to health care.[4]

44. Hebrew Prayer Book

1898–1972 | African Meeting House, Beacon Hill

Many archaeological sites contain frustratingly few artifacts giving indications of the religious affiliations of their owners. In many cases, these can be inferred from the historic record, from the relative wealth of a family at any given time, or from their cultural affiliations. For example, the refuse deposit at the Blake House could be associated with the recently arrived Irish immigrants in late nineteenth-century Dorchester, rather than with the nearby community of wealthy Protestants who had been living in the region for centuries prior to the arrival of the immigrants, because of the presence of several items of Catholic religious jewelry in the deposit.

Over the centuries, Boston's dominant religion switched from Protestant to Catholic, but this is the type of oversimplification about which archaeology can provide further insights. The African Meeting House functioned as a Baptist church from its construction in 1806 until 1898. While today the building is a museum interpreting the lives and experiences of Boston's black community, for nearly one hundred years between 1898 and 1972, the African Meeting House was the home of the Anshei Lubavitch Jewish congregation. This fragment of a Hebrew prayer book was found between the wallboards in the main sanctuary within the building (archaeology is not just about stuff dug from the ground; it is the study of the human past through artifacts *wherever* they are found). "May it be Your will Y H V H, my God and my ancestors' God, to fulfill the blemish of the 'white one' levanah [the moon], and may there be no diminishing at all in her; and may the light of the white one be like the light of the 'hot one' chamah [the sun], and like the light of the seven days of beginning creation, like it was before she was diminished, as it says 'And God formed the two great lights.'"[1]

Jews have been present in Boston since the mid-seventeenth century, but for many hundreds of years, their numbers were extremely limited. Beginning in the 1870s, a new wave of East European Jewish immigrants began arriving in the North End and establishing synagogues.[2] While these nineteenth-century synagogues have mostly been converted into other usages, street names such as Jerusalem Place and a few businesses still carry telltale evidence of the former Jewish neighborhood centered on Salem Street.

Many early Jewish communities were located in poorer areas of the city, like the West and North Ends, a typical narrative for most recently arrived immigrant communities in Boston's history (figure 44.1). The Irish and Italian communities, many of whose members were Catholic, settled in the North End and built Catholic churches.

These communities can be traced throughout Boston as they moved about the city. Around the turn of the twentieth century, the Jewish community

FIGURE 44.1
Temple Israel Jewish
Synagogue at 602
Commonwealth
Avenue in 1920
(Abdalian 1920;
photo courtesy of
the Boston Public
Library).

began spreading to Blue Hill Avenue in Roxbury, and the Irish community relocated to South Boston, as it began to be developed. The Jewish community along Blue Hill Avenue extended into the Mattapan neighborhood, but the Mattapan community was driven out by thinly veiled banking practices such as redlining, the practice of denying banking and other services or of increasing fees to certain groups of people, and blockbusting, which encouraged owners to sell at a loss by convincing them that a minority group newly arrived in a neighborhood would decrease home values. The net result of both these practices was that entire communities left well-established ethnic and religious neighborhoods, and real estate investors capitalized on the property whose value had been newly lowered. This practice continued in the West and South Ends, greatly affecting vibrant ethnic communities.

Today, many would argue that well-established communities throughout the city of Boston are being driven away from the city for exactly the opposite reason. Now that the economic outlook for Boston appears positive, home values and rents are rising quickly, causing many ethnic or religious communities with ties to specific areas of Boston to move to new locations, a practice that has been occurring in Boston (and elsewhere) for hundreds of years.

45. Lady's Wallet

1895 | Blake House Site, Dorchester

Nineteenth-century Boston saw a major change in the roles of women at home and at work. Prior to this period, most women were responsible primarily for raising children, maintaining the household, providing early education, and training daughters in domestic activities until they moved out. As the nineteenth century progressed, heightened immigration, coupled with the rise in manufacturing, resulted in an increase in poor families and in job opportunities for unskilled labor.

At the Blake House site in Dorchester, a pond filled in 1895 was excavated by then city archaeologist Ellen Berkland. It produced thousands of artifacts from a period in Dorchester's history when the neighborhood was rapidly transforming itself from large farm estates of wealthy families with extensive pedigrees to a neighborhood of multifamily three-deckers filled with first- and second-generation immigrants fleeing the cramped conditions of the North and West Ends for the relatively "new" neighborhood of Dorchester[1] (figure 45.1).

FIGURE 45.1
A 1915 view of three-deckers at 18–20 Dexter Street in Dorchester. Both structures were demolished to build Andrew Station (*Dor. Tun. Houses #18–20 Dexter St.* 1915; photo courtesy of the Boston Public Library).

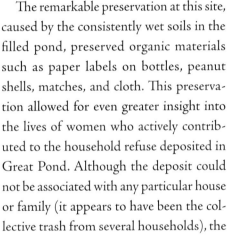

The remarkable preservation at this site, caused by the consistently wet soils in the filled pond, preserved organic materials such as paper labels on bottles, peanut shells, matches, and cloth. This preservation allowed for even greater insight into the lives of women who actively contributed to the household refuse deposited in Great Pond. Although the deposit could not be associated with any particular house or family (it appears to have been the collective trash from several households), the assemblage includes many items associated with lower-middle-class individuals and religious items identifying the former owners as Catholic. One of the challenges presented by this site was determining whether the contents of the pond fill were associated with the recently arrived Irish immigrant population or older English families still living in the area, or some combination of the two. Archaeologists were able to use the relative lack of higher-end goods, the religious artifacts, and personal possessions to show that they had come from recent immigrant families, likely Irish immigrants from the North End.[2]

Artifacts from the Blake House site, including the lady's wallet featured here, demonstrate the increasing ability, or perhaps need, of adult women to work outside the home and lead individual economic lives that could contribute to their family's financial and social success. One artifact in par-

FIGURE 45.2
Late nineteenth-
century trade card
advertising breast
milk alternatives
administered
through glass
nursing bottles and
rubber tubing (Gies
and Company
1870–1900 [ca.];
image courtesy of
the Boston Public
Library).

ticular speaks to this new reality: glass nursing bottles, several of which were recovered at the site. Along with new medicines and food products suddenly available to the public because of increasing rates of manufacturing and advertising in the 1860s, Nestlé developed one of the first baby formulas marketed specifically to women (figure 45.2) as a way to become more independent from their children and as a safer alternative to a wet nurse or to breast-feeding.[3]

These bottles and the formula they contained allowed working-class women who could not afford wet nurses (women hired to breast-feed children) to leave the home while their children were infants. Formula at this time was predominantly cow's milk, flour, and sugar, but it was sufficient to provide adequate nutrition for the thousands of children in Boston who would have been raised predominantly on the formula at the time.

Once granted this freedom, women were able to return to work or enter the workforce more quickly after giving birth. Employment allowed them to maintain or create anew an economic stream that would aid their families, now that there was another mouth to feed.

46. Comb

Circa 1870 | Paul Revere House, North End

FIGURE 46.1
Street sweepers
cleaning garbage
from a North End
street into a horse-
drawn cart in 1909.
Note the trash
barrel in the center
right (Marr 1909;
photo courtesy of
the Boston Public
Library).

As the diversity of Boston's residents increased dramatically over the course of the nineteenth and early twentieth centuries, self-identity began to be expressed more outwardly through material goods. In many ways, the narrative of Boston became the narrative of the "other" in the late nineteenth century. After several generations, this "other" has become the norm, as Irish, Italian, and black communities dominate the cultural presence in Boston. This radical switch in population and power was accompanied by struggles for acceptance and community preservation. The black community in Beacon Hill responded to the outward discrimination and lack of access to public resources in the relatively open Boston community by founding their own societies, including the African Masonic Lodge, the African Society, and the African-American Female Intelligence Community.[1] These groups not only solidified community identity, but filled vital needs of the community they served.

Irish immigrants who flooded into Boston in the mid-nineteenth century brought with them their religion, cultural practices, and identity. These were often represented through religious and political statements and Irish iconography, including the Irish harp and "Home Rule" pipes representing Irish demands for more self-regulation.[2]

The incredible density of immigrants living in poor conditions in the North End neighborhood produced a very negative opinion of the area and its residents among both wealthier Boston residents and visitors to the city. Although the city attempted to combat rubbish buildup in the streets (figure 46.1), it did not do so frequently enough to keep up with the accumulation, and many personal and household refuse items were tossed into already overflowing outhouses. The smell and unsightly trash in the North End did not improve the area's reputation, and the overall lack of concern for the immigrants' living conditions on the part of predatory tenement owners, the lack of enforcement of sanitary laws, and the infrequent and unreliable trash collection were the fundamental cause of the rubbish problem—not the immigrants themselves, who were struggling daily to rise above their living conditions in one of the only neighborhoods affordable and open to them.

The North Square area, where Paul Revere's house is located, was dominated in the nineteenth century by Italians from the Avellino province of Italy. During this time, the Paul Revere House would have been a tenement for dozens of recently arrived immigrants. In the 1890s, Italian and Jewish immigrants flocked to the neighborhood, and all three groups lived there in relatively equal numbers at the turn of the twentieth century. Although historic photos of the period do not generally identify people by their name or ethnicity, the artifacts they left behind do.

Boston University archaeologists excavating behind the Revere house in the 1980s revealed the small Bakelite comb shown in the main photo, a mundane item by many people's standards and a common artifact from nineteenth-century archaeological sites. It was recovered along with several lice combs from an outhouse behind the building.[3] Irish immigrants and their children poured into the North End, where this comb was found, after the potato famine in the 1850s. The density of families in this neighborhood and within the individual tenement rooms throughout the North End resulted in the need for people to protect their goods. It is likely that the comb in the main photo was one of the owner's few personal possessions. This comb is a portion of a larger comb that had broken in the past, and from which several comb teeth had been lost (or removed); the remaining "handle" was then smoothed to make combing with the broken plastic item more comfortable. Despite this damage, the owner, "W+ KeLLe[y?]," valued it enough to sign it, marking it as his or her own to keep it away from the hands of the many other adults or children who were also living in that probably overcrowded and busy tenement, in what was once the home owned by Paul Revere. We have yet to determine if the name is someone's first initial and last name, or if it represents a love note linking two individuals' names with a plus sign.

Dozens of children would have passed through the Paul Revere tenement house, just as they would have through the many hundreds of similar buildings in the North End and elsewhere. These children would be educated in public schools (figure 46.2) and would become the first generation of immigrants in Boston to rise in prominence through both numbers and political power, despite their modest upbringing. This immigrant story is a common one, repeated throughout Boston's history to the present day.

New immigrants and those whose families had called Boston home for centuries all went through a period of transition around the turn of the twentieth century. Members of each group retained aspects of their lives just as they had been in previous decades, but the movements of the immigrants at this time, whether across town or across the Atlantic, brought with them opportunities to adopt new identities. Some chose to represent themselves through their past associations, others formed new identities and social organizations to redefine themselves and their communities, and still others simply identified themselves by a name on a comb. Together, the people of Boston at the turn of the twentieth century created a diverse and vibrant community that was not only greater than the sum of its parts, but defined by that very diversity.

47. Red Sox Pin

1912 | Dillaway-Thomas House, Roxbury

While Boston at the turn of the century was quickly becoming a melting pot of people from a variety of locations around the world, then as now, few things brought the Boston community together like sports (figure 47.1). Baseball was rapidly becoming an American pastime. In 1900, the newly formed American League created a franchise in Boston called the Boston Americans.[1]

By 1901, a Major League–size baseball diamond and stands arose on Huntington Avenue, an area now within the grounds of Northeastern University. The first modern World Series was held on the same spot between the Boston Americans and the Pittsburgh Pirates. Players of this series included baseball legends Cy Young and Honus Wagner. The first three games in the best-of-nine game series were held in Boston, where the Americans lost two of the three. The series moved to Pittsburgh, where Boston lost again. Boston went into the fourth game down three games to one, won, and had a winning streak. On October 13, 1903, the Americans returned to Boston, where they clinched their fifth game, the fourth in a row, solidifying their lead and winning the first World Series.[2]

Managers of the Americans switched the team stockings to red in 1907 after a league color change, which resulted in the nickname Boston Red Sox, one that would stick with the team from then on.[3] Fenway Park opened April 9, 1912, in a marshy area known as the Fens; in its very first year it hosted the Boston Red Sox as they won the final game of the 1912 World Series. Only

two years later the Red Sox would once again head to the World Series, soon losing at Fenway and starting a decades-long losing trend (figure 47.2).

In the early 1900s, the Fenway area was relatively undeveloped, having only recently been made into firm ground, thanks to the filling in of the Back Bay and the lower tidal areas near Kenmore Square. Today, you can still see the reeds and wetlands around Stony Brook near Fenway, and nearby construction often turns up the foul-smelling wetland soils that lie beneath Fenway and the surrounding area.

Red Sox fans were and always will be a complete cross-section of Boston residents of all economic backgrounds. After a string of victories in 1910s, the joy of a World Series title would remain elusive—it was eighty-six years before the Red Sox won again in 2004.

Owners and managers of baseball teams around the world understand the need for fan loyalty and the value of marketing and merchandising teams, and they understood this even in the early twentieth century. During the archaeological excavations in front of the Dillaway-Thomas house in Roxbury,[4] archaeologists uncovered the small piece of cast white metal shown in the main photo. This was a pin made by the Red Sox organization and given to children who were fans of the team. The pin measures only about one inch in length, and when it was complete, it was a pseudo-humanoid figure consisting of a baseball face, a body made of a catcher's pads, and arms and legs composed of crossed baseball bats. One surviving example with a brightly painted surface has survived, with the date 1912 on the lower portion. This "FAN KID" pin was likely given out in celebration of a Red Sox win or the opening of the new stadium.

Today, Fenway Park is the oldest standing baseball field in Major League Baseball, and every year the owners of the team, managers of the stadium, engineers, and the preservation community work together to ensure that the historic character of the park is maintained, while it meets the needs of the team and fans alike.

FIGURE 47.2
A 1914 view of Fenway Park during the World Series (Bond 1914; photo courtesy of the Boston Public Library).

48. Cop and Robber Toy and Bell

1920–1940 | Brook Farm, West Roxbury

Children are rarely present in the historic record, apart from their names and ages, if that. Many archaeologists rely on tax and census records for names and ages of those who lived on the sites they excavate. Early tax records in Boston do not include women or children, and census records tally occupants only every ten years, thus leaving many out of the records entirely.

The combination of children wanting entertainment and parents desiring to keep them from getting in the way has meant that for thousands of years people have been making toys (artifact 22). Also for thousands of years, children have been breaking and losing toys. Their loss is history's gain. These artifacts provide rare insights into the lives of children, who, as mentioned, rarely if ever make it into recorded history.

Although life was very different for children in the past, play and fun have always been a priority throughout human history. Since many archaeological sites are associated with the rear of buildings, where most children's activities typically took place, toys and other artifacts associated with children are often found.

At the Clough House site that the City Archaeology Program excavated on behalf of the Old North Church Foundation in 2013, numerous drainage features, such as cisterns and pipes, were encountered as the excavations progressed. At the bottom of each of these drains were numerous marbles and other small, round objects that had fallen in and been lost—at least until the archaeologists came along. We can imagine that the children probably attempted to retrieve their lost toys, no doubt employing creative contraptions to fish them from the drains before giving up, but the young owners could hardly have expected that the toys would be recovered only after the backyard had been excavated by a bunch of scientists looking for items lost by children, in order to write about the history of their lives.

At the same site, numerous fragments of dolls were recovered. Parts of tea sets were also found in three sizes: standard, child, and doll. Child tea sets were nearly identical to adult versions, though typically a bit poorer-quality and smaller in scale, but still fully functional. These sets would allow girls in the eighteenth and nineteenth centuries to learn and practice proper tea etiquette, a requirement for many women who wanted to follow the social norms of the time, have successful families, and make households of their own. Doll tea sets were another notch smaller. A tiny complete teacup, far too small for the hands of a child, showed that girls in nineteenth-century Boston not only learned tea etiquette themselves but at a very young age were teaching their dolls these same principles, as they later would their own daughters.

Toy guns, a bow and arrow, shovels, and toy trains have also been found

FIGURE 48.1
Children of
the North End
Mission orphanage
at the end of the
nineteenth century.
Note the material
culture possessed
by the children,
including their
clothing and dolls
(*A Window Pull*,
1868–1902 [ca.];
photo courtesy of
the Boston Public
Library).

FIGURE 48.2
Late nineteenth-
century view of
the former Mt.
Hope Home in
Jamaica Plain, a
contemporary
orphanage to the
Brook Farm Home
(*Mt. Hope Home*,
1868–1902 [ca.];
photo courtesy of
the Boston Public
Library).

on sites from Charlestown to West Roxbury. These artifacts show that while the girls were practicing "proper" feminine traditions, boys were also expected to learn or conform to typical masculine standards of their time.

At the Brook Farm site previously mentioned in artifacts 38 and 39, an orphanage that operated on the property between 1822 and 1977 was excavated as part the larger investigation. Hundreds of children would have called this place home over the years, with the result that numerous toys and children's objects were left in the yards of the buildings. Orphanages were common throughout Boston (figure 48.1), and the artifacts featured in the main photo illustrate nicely a snapshot in one of these children's lives (figure 48.2).

The "cop and robber" cast-lead toys were found just below the grass layer, hidden under the iron dome of an old-fashioned school bell. The child who was playing with these toys likely hid them under the bell, probably to keep them away from the other children at the orphanage or to keep the toys safe until the next time the child returned to the yard to play. Archaeologists call this *caching*, and it is evident on sites all over Boston, and beyond, from Native American camps to seventeenth-century basements to twentieth-century orphanages. People may change, and cultures may come and go, but human nature has remained fundamentally unchanged for much of history.

49. Lipstick

Circa 1940–1950 | Clough House Site, North End

Now that we're near the end, let's ask an obvious, and perhaps overdue, question: What is archaeology? Many reading this may find that the more recent artifacts featured seem "less archaeological" than those from the earlier portions of the book. *Archaeology,* as we archaeologists describe it, is simply the study of the human past through the artifacts that people leave behind. One important thing missing from this definition is a cutoff date—the coin dropped today is already part of the archaeological record. When I encounter people who doubt this fact, I always remind them that archaeology is not about the stuff; it is about the story. We may know more about the story of daily life now because we live in the "now" and can see how many things interconnect in someone's life, but over time, these connections break down and the meanings behind various aspects of the past are lost.

The lipstick shown in the main photo is a perfect example. Recovered from the Clough House site in the North End in 2013, it is one of the few artifacts in this book that is from a dig that I have had the pleasure of personally organizing. The Clough House was built in 1712, was expanded in 1806 to become a tenement for immigrants, and today is a museum that houses a print shop and a chocolate store,

FIGURE 49.1
A Boston woman in patriotic clothing during World War II. Note the deep color of her lipstick, possibly similar in hue to the lipstick recovered at the Clough House site (Jones 1939–1945 [ca.]; photo courtesy of the Boston Public Library, Leslie Jones Collection).

and is the home of the Old North Church's sexton. But that is the history of the *house,* and a house is a place where people live. This lipstick was purchased by someone, most likely a woman, in the 1940s, during the period when Boston was experiencing World War II (figures 49.1 and 49.2). When it was first found, we thought it was some sort of bullet casing, but once it was cleaned at the lab we could see the extending knob on the bottom and realized it might be a lipstick case. We carefully pulled off the cap, not only exposing the bright-red hue of the lipstick but also releasing a blast of makeup odor. Rarely—outside a privy—do we have the opportunity to experience, firsthand, the smell of an artifact or a time period. The person who last used this makeup was probably trying to emulate the makeup styles of the wartime 1940s and 1950s in which pale faces and boldly colored lips dominated pop culture. How did it get outside? Well, it was certainly not tossed out with the chamber pot contents. More than likely it ended up there just as most of the current artifacts we leave behind in yards and parks do: it was dropped

accidentally. While the story may not be the oldest one told in this book, it nevertheless is a story of the human past, and it captures a brief glimpse into the life of someone from a time before now, during a period of major change in Boston and the country as a whole.

What does archaeology of today look like? We concentrate our garbage in trash bags that are driven to places to be buried or burned. We do not throw away nearly as much garbage in our yards or bathrooms as was done in the past, yet we now use many more objects that do not decompose. We actively recycle, and there are public trash cans throughout Boston to prevent further archaeological contributions to the parks and public spaces we get to enjoy, yet cigarette butts and bits of trash are visible everywhere if you look for them. More important, do we need archaeology in the future? Sure, we can always engage in archaeology of the deep past, but with digital media recording our every thought and idea and with more books and documents being produced now than ever before, will we have mysteries of the past that still need to be solved through digging? I do not have a good answer for that, but I will be the first to state that archaeology is good fun and will persist as long as there are questions about the past to answer.

50. Showtime Token

1960–1984 | Boston Common, Downtown

In my opinion, one of archaeology's greatest contributions to the study of the past is its ability to cut through the clutter of accepted narratives and *la vie en rose* stories of the past and reveal what *actually* happened in a given place at a given time. While Boston's contribution to official history is known the world over, numerous examples of a seedy past reveal a darker underbelly to Boston that is every bit as much a part of its story (artifact 40, for example). Archaeology does not whitewash history, and this book will not, either.

This peep-show token, good for "one play only," was excavated from the Common during its archaeological survey in 1987. Undoubtedly, it originated in Boston's legendary "Combat Zone" nearby, an area with a unique history that epitomizes the changes in Boston's image over the past forty years.

The red-light district formerly centered on North Street in the North End (again, see artifact 40) relocated to Scollay Square in the early 1900s, transforming a downtown neighborhood of hotels, opera houses, and theaters into the "crossroads of hell," with burlesque houses and cheap rental accommodations catering to the steady flow of sailors from the Charlestown Navy Yard, the wealthier businessmen from the nearby offices, and local college students.[1] Despite the outcry of many, Scollay Square's sex industry services were in high demand. The resulting decline in property values in the center of downtown Boston attracted political attention.

FIGURE 50.1
A 1904 view of 658 Washington Street, future center of the Combat Zone and home of the infamous Pilgrim and Naked I theaters (photo courtesy of the City of Boston Archives).

FIGURE 50.2
A 1960s view of the
Pilgrim Theater
marquee. Note
that the portion
of the building in
figure 50.1 (658
Washington Street)
is visible on the left
side of the marquee
(photo courtesy
of the City of
Boston Archives).

In 1959, John Collins was elected mayor of Boston. He continued a period
of extensive redevelopment of significant portions of Boston often referred to
as urban renewal. Urban-renewal projects had already radically transformed
the landscape and populations of the West End and the New York Street
area of the South End, in the name of improving Boston's failing economy,
but clear undercurrents of racism were also evident, along with a desire to rid
Boston neighborhoods of minorities, to stem the drain of upper-class white
residents to Boston's suburbs.

Mayor Collins's urban-renewal plans included the creation of the Boston
Redevelopment Authority (BRA), the development of the Prudential Center
in the Back Bay, and the razing of Scollay Square in the early 1960s to make
way for the development of the Government Center complex.[2] Although the
intent of this redevelopment was to rid the area of the sex industry, it did not
reduce the demand. As a result, the district relocated less than one mile away,
to Washington Street, where low rents and the proximity to downtown created
conditions similarly favorable to those at Scollay Square (figures 50.1 and 50.2).

The area would become known as the Combat Zone, owing to its notoriety
for crime, violence, and the omnipresent uniformed soldiers who gave the area
a military appearance. The dramatic rise of topless bars, adult movie theaters
(where the token likely originated), adult bookstores, and prostitution drew
great media, police, and political attention. The striking down of obscenity
laws by the Supreme Court in 1974 led to near impunity for these businesses.

The BRA, in an attempt to combat the Combat Zone without encouraging it to disperse or relocate as it had after Scollay Square, devised an "Adult Entertainment District" that formally defined, through zoning, the area along Washington Street between Essex and Kneeland Streets within which these establishments could operate without legal opposition. This plan included the redesignation of the Combat Zone as "Liberty Tree Park"—so named after the Revolutionary War–era tree that once stood within the district. It also envisaged greater enforcement of antiprostitution laws and improvement within the district of such infrastructure as lighting and sidewalks, in the hope of increasing property values while containing the spread of these businesses.[3]

Although the tiny park was created within the district and improvements were made, local business owners were less willing than expected to maintain and improve the outward appearance of the buildings containing the various establishments, and a lack of law enforcement against prostitution resulted in the open acceptance of its presence and a dramatic rise in its practice.[4]

The Combat Zone's end came about gradually over the latter half of the 1970s. In 1976, the release of an internal report condemning the lack of police enforcement of the area, the resignation and hiring of a new police commissioner, and the murder of a Harvard football player drew renewed cries for improvements.[5] An immediate police crackdown on illegal activities quickly fizzled, and the Combat Zone continued to thrive.

In the end, a development boom in the surrounding area; the invention of the VCR, which allowed adult-movie viewing at home; and the rise of adult-entertainment businesses in surrounding communities eroded the economic stability of the Combat Zone. The election of Raymond Flynn as mayor of Boston in 1983 brought with it a renewed desire to complete the erosion of the district. Large land purchases encouraged by Mayor Flynn and the BRA in 1984 resulted in the eviction and redevelopment of many of the Combat Zone's remaining keystone institutions.[6]

Like many areas of Boston in the 1980s and early 1990s, the Combat Zone was "cleaned up" through the radical transformation of buildings, landscape, and infrastructure. These include the removal of the elevated railroad system and the Route 93 elevated highway (triggering the archaeological surveys before the Big Dig), and more recently the transformation of the Seaport district in South Boston. All of these changes have been made for the economic benefit of Boston, but always at the expense of someone or something, whether it is an industry, a community, or a general cultural "vibe." As we look back on the history of Boston, it is this constant flux of places, people, and vibes that defines both its greatness and its contributions to an overall historic narrative.

CONCLUSION. The Future of Archaeology in Boston

Around the world, archaeology is under threat, and in Boston it is no different. The rise of television programs promoting the looting of archaeological sites, as well as development and climate change, are actively eliminating the historical data stored within the ground. Archaeological sites are nonrenewable resources. When they are damaged or destroyed, they can never come back. Archaeological excavation destroys a site as it is dug, and that is why it is absolutely critical that all archaeological work be conducted by a trained professional who will ensure that the archaeological data are properly recorded in the field, notes are taken, drawings are made, artifacts are properly processed at the lab and curated, reports are written, and the collections and information are made available to the public, so that everyone can benefit from the history that is produced from the archaeological record.

The state of archaeology in Boston is growing but under threat. The very real fact of climate change is the greatest natural hazard we face, bringing storm surges, violent weather, and the gradual increase in sea levels. These changes threaten low-lying areas and our Harbor Islands, which contain some of the most important archaeological sites in the city. As I work to preserve, protect, and promote the archaeology of Boston, I seek out partnerships with donors, volunteers, and the general public, without whose support the City Archaeology Program could vanish. The artifacts discussed in this book represent just a tiny portion of the unique and irreplaceable archaeological heritage of the city of Boston, but they demonstrate the great promise of archaeology and its ability to bring history to life.

1. Mattapan Banded Rhyolite, 4.8 × 2.8 × 2.2 cm, Mattapan Quarry, Babson Street and Cookson Terrace, Mattapan.

   Fluted Point, 7.3 × 2.8 cm, Monomoy National Wildlife Sanctuary, Chatham.

2. Neville Point, 4.4 × 3.1 cm, Boston Common, Unit 27.1 expanded, Str 2 Lev 2, 20–30 cmbs, Catalog #B1.0228.

3. Fishweir Stakes, 18 × 9 cm (jar), found in the 1940s in Back Bay during construction.

4. Native Pottery, 4.7 × 3.4 × 1.2 cm, Boston Common, Unit 27.N24.5 W20, Str 3 Lev 2, 180–208 cmbs, Catalog #B1.0985.

   Incised Native Pottery, 2 × 1.8 × 0.4 cm, Boston Common, Unit 79.21, Str 1 Lev 3, 28 cmbs, Catalog #B1.0895.

5. Fish Spear, 5.5 × 0.8 cm, Spectacle Island, Site number 19 SU 38, Unit N11 W3, Lev 4A, Catalog #11,120.

   Shells, Boston Common, Unit 27.1, Str IV Lev 1, 56–66 cmbs, Catalog #B1.0069.

6. Massachusett Weaving, 16 × 9 cm, found by construction worker in the vicinity of 470 Atlantic Avenue, 19 feet below ground.

7. Arrowhead, 4.3 × 2 cm, Boston Common, Unit 19.152834, Str 2 Lev 1, 23–33 cmbs, Catalog #B1.0093.

   Levanna Point, 2.7 × 2.5 cm, Boston Common, Unit 45.5, Str 3 Lev 1, 50–60 cmbs, Catalog #B1.0588.

8. Trade Weight, 6 × 6 × 0.5 cm, Lovell Island, Boston Harbor.

9. Stone from Great House, 12.5 × 8.5 × 10 cm, City Square Archaeological District, Unit 55, N6 E14, Feature 192, Strata A Level 3, 20–30 cmbs.

10. Portuguese Plate, 11 × 7.5 cm, James Garrett site, Feature 43, Provenience #M.1278, M.1281, M.0332, and M.0900.

    Various Ceramics, James Garrett site, Feature 43.

11. Chamber Pot, 19.5 × 15 cm, Cross Street Backlot, Feature 4, Provenience 138, Lev 6–8, Catalog #36,416.

12. Whipworm Egg, ~60 × 30 microns, Cross Street Backlot, Feature 4.

    Lice Comb, 5 × 1.8 cm, Cross Street Backlot, Feature 4, Catalog #35,254.

13. Sleeve, 17 × 20 cm, Cross Street Backlot, EU 140.9, Feature 4, Catalog #38,129.

14. Bowling Ball, 11 × 7.5 cm, Cross Street Backlot, HA-13 6488, EU 141.2, Harris Matrix Number (HN) 100, Catalog #35,795.

15. Plate, 7.3 × 17 cm, Cross Street Backlot, Feature 4, Phase 1-5.

16. Child's Shoe, 17 × 12.5 cm, Cross Street Backlot, Bag 6405, EU 138, Feature 4 Level 1, HN 100, Catalog #35,985-9.

17. Fruit Pits, Cross Street Backlot, Feature 4, Unit 138.8, HN148.

    Earthenware Pot, 30 × 22 cm, Cross Street Backlot, Feature 4, Provenience 141.2.

18. Bellarmine Bottle, 11 × 15 cm, Cross Street Backlot, Feature 4, Phase 1-10, Vessel #1195.

    Pig Skull, 19 × 9.5 cm, Cross Street Backlot, Feature 4, Bag 6744.

19. Lace, 20 × 1.5 cm, Cross Street Backlot, EU 140.4, Feature 4, Level 4, Catalog #38,120.

    Thimble and Pins, Cross Street Backlot, Thimble: Prov 141 Lev 2, Pins: Prov 138 Lev 7,8.

20. Red-Clay Pipe, 4.3 × 4.5 cm, Paddy's Alley, HA12, EU 4 Lev 3, HN 31F.

    Colonoware, 16.5 × 16.5 cm, Cross Street Backlot, HA 13, 6035, Unit 26.1, Feature 1.

21. Cat Skeleton, City Square Archaeological District, U42, Feature 193.

22. Whizzer, 4.9 × 4.9 cm, Faneuil Hall, Bot 8 NW Quad, S-V L-2, FS 19, Rec #5 C-063.

    Gaming Token, 1.5 × 1.5 × 0.4 cm, Clough House, Unit C1, Str 4 Lev 8 70–80 cm, MATS #54689.

23. Porcelain Tea Bowl, 7 × 3.8 cm, City Square Archaeological District, Unit 9 Feature 141, Vessel 63.

    Porcelain Saucer, 11.5 × 1.5 cm, City Square Archaeological District, Unit 47 Feature 141, Vessel 35.

    Lead Seal, 3 × 2.2 cm, Faneuil Hall, Provenience B 21.60, Catalog #3384.

    Staffordshire Slipware Posset Pot, 23 × 14 cm, 16 cm opening, City Square Archaeological District, Unit 3 and 62, Feature 177, Vessel 80.

24. Redware Waster, 14 × 10 × 6.5 cm, Parker-Harris Pottery.

    Fused Mug, Trivet, and Chamber Pot Rim, 13 × 7 cm, Parker-Harris Pottery.

25. Parker-Harris Mug, 10.5 × 16.5 cm, Parker-Harris Site, U 7, NO E2, Feature 96, Level 15, 16, Strata A, 140–160 cm, Vessel 110.

    Chamber Pot, 21 × 22 cm, City Square Archaeological District, Unit 62, Feature 177, Vessel 78.

26. Bottle Seal, 4.6 × 4.4 mm, Paddy's Alley Site, HA-12, EU 17 Level 7, Catalog #24,641.

    Wine Bottle, 22 × 10 cm, City Square Archaeological District, Unit 47, S2 W6, Str F Lev 21, 200–210 cmbs, Feature 142.

27. Soldering Iron, 9.5 × 1.4 cm, Paddy's Alley, HA 12, EU 9.5, Catalog #24,714.

28. Teapot, 17 × 9 cm, City Square Archaeological District, U47, Feature 142, Lev 18 Strata E, Vessel 7.

29. Gunflint, 25–30 cm, Boston Common, Unit 79.4, Str 3 Lev 2, Catalog #B1.0582.

    Musket Ball, 1.7 cm, Boston Common, Unit 79.4, Str 2 Lev 2, 25–30 cmbs.

30. Bar Shot, 19 × 7.7 cm, City Square Archaeological District.

    Cannonball, 7.7 × 7.7 cm, City Square Archaeological District.

31. Charcoal, City Square Archaeological District, Unit 17, S10 W4, Feature 80, Str A Lev 3, 28–30 cmbs.

32. Powder House Brick, 15 × 8.5 × 5 cm, Boston Common, Flagstaff Hill, Block 10.

33. Massachusetts Cent, 3 × 3 cm, Boston Common, Unit 27 N24.5 W. 30, Lev 2 Str 8, 80–90 cmbs, Catalog #B1.0893.

34. Sail Needle, 0.5 × 3.5 cm, City Square Archaeological District, Unit 50, S4 E16, Feature 164, 36–40 cmbs, Str A Lev 4.

35. Tortoiseshell Comb, 6.7 × 0.4 cm, Boston Common, Unit 8, Str 6 Lev 3, 110–120 cmbs, Catalog #B1.1028.

36. Shell-Edge Pearlware, 10.7 × 5.5 cm, African Meeting House, Context #AMH 130, Vessel 2794.

37. Cowbell, 7.8 × 7.5 cm, Boston Common, Unit 27.7, Strata 1, 1–55 cmbs.

38. Nib, 3.6 × 0.5 cm, Brook Farm Site, Hive, N30 E13, Str 4 Lev 4, Catalog #B19.1663.

39. New York Militia Button, 2.5 × 2.4 cm, Brook Farm Site, Hive, N21 E 1, 55–45 cmbs, Str 1 Lev 2.

40. Vaginal Syringe, 15.3 × 2.0 cm, Endicott Street Privy, BOS HA 14, Bag #8662, Feature 38, HN 230

    Plunger, 16.7 × 2.4 cm, Endicott Street Privy, BOS HA 14, Bag #8668, Feature 38, HN 234, Artifact #38,954.

    Millstone Fragment, 126 × 67 cm, Mill Pond.

    Copaiba Oil Bottle, 8.3 × 3 cm, Endicott Street Privy, BOS HA 14, Bag #8709, Feature 38, HN 235, Artifact #39,623.

41. Love Token, 2.2 × 2.2 cm, Boston Common.

42. Horse Blinder, Metropolitan Horse Railroad, Leather Deposit, Test Trenches 7, 12, 23, and 27.

43. Rock and Tar Bottle, 9 × 3 cm, Blake House, Trench 1 Unit D, BG #0352.

44. Hebrew Prayer Book, 9.1 × 4.5 cm, found October 18, 1984, in sanctuary at west wall behind wainscot at southern corner wedged behind wooden support for later pews.

45. Lady's Wallet, 13.5 × 8.3 cm (closed), Blake House, Unit C, Lev 8, Catalog #BH1909.

46. Comb, 9 × 4.5 cm, Paul Revere House, Unit E17/19/21, Lower privy fill.

47. Red Sox Pin, 2 × 2 cm, Dillaway-Thomas House, Unit 24, Provenience 89, 13–20 cmbs.

48. Cop and Robber Toy and Bell, 5.5 × 3 cm (toy), 8.8 × 3 cm (bell), Brook Farm, Hive, Transect A TP 1–5, Catalog #B19.0045.

49. Lipstick, 3.8 × 1.3 cm, Clough House, Unit C6, Str 2 Lev 2, 10–20 cmbs, MATS #51088.

50. Showtime Token, 2.2 × 2.2 cm, Boston Common, Unit 79.153134, Str 1 Level 1, 0–9 cmbs, B1.0303.

Notes

INTRODUCTION

1. Jeffries Wyman: Browman and Williams 2013, 286; Frederic Putnam: Browman and Williams 2013, 67.

2. Charles Willoughby: Browman and Williams 2013, 209; Peabody Museum: Hooton 1943, 235; Harvard's archaeological collections: Hooton 1943.

3. Boylston Street fishweirs: Johnson 1942; Frederick Johnson: Johnson 1942.

4. Charles River Basin: Dincauze 1968; Boston Harbor islands: Luedtke 1975.

5. Bower 1986; Bower and Rushing 1979.

6. Bower and Rushing 1979.

7. Bower and Rushing 1979.

8. Historic and Native sites: Elia et al. 1989; the entire route of the tunnel: Edens and Kingsley 1998.

9. Bradley et al. 1982, 244.

10. Mrozowski 1985.

PART I. SHAWMUT

1. Lothrop et al. 2011.

1. MATTAPAN BANDED RHYOLITE

1. Saugus: Grimes et al. 1984; Wakefield: archaeological site data on file at the Massachusetts Historical Commission; Canton: Donta 2006.

2. Oldest datable site: Ritchie et al. 1984; Long Island and Deer Island: Ritchie et al. 1984.

2. NEVILLE POINT

1. Pendery 1988.

2. Doucette and Cross 1997.

3. Skehan 2001.

3. FISHWEIR STAKES

1. Johnson 1942.

2. Decima and Dincauze 1998.

4. NATIVE POTTERY

1. Pendery 1988.

5. FISH SPEAR

1. Edens and Kingsley 1998.

7. ARROWHEAD

1. The Great Elm: Bonner 1722; the city of Boston lacked trees: Wood 1993.

8. TRADE WEIGHT

1. Dooley-Fairchild 2014.

9. STONE FROM GREAT HOUSE

1. Moore 1848.

2. Hunnewell 1915.

3. Gallagher et al. 1994.

4. City of Boston 1992.

10. PORTUGUESE PLATE

1. Wyman 1879.

2. Pendery et al. 1984.

3. Pendery 1992.

11. CHAMBER POT

1. Elia et al. 1989.

2. Cook and Balicki 1998.

3. Robert Nanny: Savage 1873 and Quint 1879; Katherine Wheelwright: Quint 1879.

4. Robert left his estate: Suffolk County Probate Records, no. 348; Katherine remarried: Boston Town Records, 1660–1701.

5. Suffolk County Probate Records, no. 3718.

12. WHIPWORM EGG

1. Ministers were the primary health providers: Hughes 1957; miasmas: Bridenbaug 1955.

2. Cook and Balicki 1998.

3. Worm expellants: Culpeper 1992; believed at the time to treat: Culpeper 1992.

4. Mumcuoglu 2008.

13. SLEEVE

1. Ulrich 1982.

2. Bowditch 1827–1859.

3. Ulrich 1982.

4. Ulrich 1982.

5. Cook and Balicki 1998.

14. BOWLING BALL

1. Cook and Balicki 1998.

2. Cook and Balicki 1998.

15. PLATE

1. First woman to legally divorce: Cook 1998; privy dates: Cook and Balicki 1998.

2. The exact details: Superior Court of Suffolk County 1671, 12:63; numerous examples of physical abuse: Superior Court of Suffolk County 1671, 12:63; repeatedly threw and kicked: Cook and Balicki 1998, 57.

3. Edward's adulterous behavior: Superior Court of Suffolk County 1671, 12:60; Mary Read: Cook and Balicki 1998, 56; Mary later gave birth: Cook and Balicki 1998, 56; local innkeepers also testified: Cook and Balicki 1998, 57; Mary Moore and Hannah Allen: Superior Court of Suffolk County 1671, 12:66; Edward was too drunk: Superior Court of Suffolk County 1671, 12:66.

4. Superior Court of Suffolk County 1671, 12:63.

5. Edward was found guilty: Superior Court of Suffolk County 1671, 12:60 and Cook and Balicki 1998, 57; Katherine lived as a single woman: Cook and Balicki 1998, 57; she lived with an unrelated couple: Cook and Balicki 1998, 58; upon her death: Cook and Balicki 1998, 58.

16. CHILD'S SHOE

1. Plymouth Ancestors, 2010 (ca.).

2. Plymouth Ancestors, 2010 (ca.).

3. Cook and Balicki 1998.

17. FRUIT PITS

1. Over 9,000 pieces of bone: Cook and Balicki 1998; Puritan Boston diet: Landon 1996.

2. Cook and Balicki 1998, 153.

3. Cows were butchered nearby: Cook and Balicki 1998, 209; the family ate other animals: Cook and Balicki 1998, 209–210.

4. Plants played a significant role: Cook and Balicki 1998, 210; plant types: Cook and Balicki 1998, 210; stone fruit: Cook and Balicki 1998, 210.

18. BELLARMINE BOTTLE

1. Cook and Balicki 1998.

2. Cook and Balicki 1998, 229.

19. LACE

1. Colonial Laws of Massachusetts 1651.

20. RED-CLAY PIPE

1. At least fourteen Africans or African Americans: Cook and Balicki 1998, 239; the Lake family had a slave: Cook and Balicki 1998, 239.

PART 3. FROM COLONIST TO REBEL (1700–1775)

1. Mather 2009.

21. CAT SKELETON

1. Gallagher et al. 1994.

2. Merrifield 1988.

22. WHIZZER

1. Whizzer: Stone 1974, 154; made from a musket ball: Neumann and Kravick 1975, 127.

2. Cassedy et al. 2013, 87.

3. Cassedy et al. 2013, 94; Fiske 1898, 143.

4. Thomas took over as paymaster: Stark 1907, 351; he was banished: Stark 1907, 137.

24. REDWARE WASTER

1. Gallagher et al. 1992.

25. PARKER-HARRIS MUG

1. Founded a pottery: Gallagher et al. 1992, 9; Grace's husband died: Gallagher et al. 1992, 20.
2. Shammas 1994, 9.

26. BOTTLE SEAL

1. John Carnes was born: Proceedings of the Massachusetts Historical Society 1918 and Cook and Balicki 1998, 48; John married Sarah Baker: Roberts 1895, 454; moved to Paddy's Alley: Cook and Balicki 1998, 48.
2. Cook and Balicki 1998.
3. John married a third time: Roberts 1895, 54; John was incredibly wealthy: Shipton 1960, 137.

27. SOLDERING IRON

1. Hull 1992.
2. Museum of Fine Arts 1916, 46.
3. Museum of Fine Arts 1916, 46.

28. TEAPOT

1. Noel Hume 2001, 125.
2. Walsh 1892.

PART 4. CONFLICT AND WAR (1765–1783)

1. British Parliament 1765.

30. BAR SHOT

1. Frothingham 1890.
2. Frothingham 1890, 123.
3. Frothingham 1890, 125.
4. Frothingham 1890, 126–127.
5. Frothingham 1890, 143.

31. CHARCOAL

1. Bacon 1892, 115.
2. Insurance values: Bacon 1892, 116; soil and surrounding artifacts were pushed: Edes 1880, 548.
3. Gallagher et al. 1994, 44.
4. Gallagher et al. 1994, 44.

PART 5. A CHANGING CITY IN A CHANGING WORLD (1780–1983)

1. Farrell 1993.
2. Farrell 1993, 22.
3. Passenger Manifest Lists 1841–1891.
4. Clapp 1916, 140.

33. MASSACHUSETTS CENT

1. Carr 2005, 151.
2. Carr 2005.
3. Ward 2001, 161.
4. Jefferson 1784.

34. SAIL NEEDLE

1. Library of Congress 1807.
2. An Act Declaring War 1812.
3. Hickey 1989.
4. Lyman 1823.

35. TORTOISESHELL COMB

1. Clements 1993.
2. Stokinger and Moran 1978.

36. SHELL-EDGE PEARLWARE

1. Jaynes 2005, 27.
2. Bower 1986; Landon 2007.
3. Bower 1986, 58.
4. Domingo was a caterer: Bower 1986, 58; he was responsible for: Bower 1986, 58; nearly matching dishes: Landon 2007, 17.

37. COWBELL

1. Boston Town Records 1646.
2. Barber 1916, 146.

38. NIB

1. Ticknor 1913.
2. Formed a utopian community: Delano 2009, 1; most celebrated utopian experiment: Delano 2009, 2.
3. McFarland 2004, 149.
4. Delano 2009, 256.

39. NEW YORK MILITIA BUTTON

1. Massachusetts sent: Schouler 1868, 667, 613; Massachusetts Fifty-Fourth: Emilio 1894; Camp Meigs: Emilio 1894, 19; the regiment left Boston: Emilio 1894, 31; headed north to Battery Wharf: Emilio 1894, 32.

2. Second Massachusetts Infantry Regiment: Bruce 1906, 14; formerly the Brook Farm utopian community: Cox 2013, 45.

3. Robert Gould Shaw: Cox 2013, 47; militia coat: Shaw 1861.

40. VAGINAL SYRINGE

1. Duis 1999, 235.

2. Mrs. Lake was the madam: Laskowski 2011; privy escaped disturbance: Laskowski 2011; Mill Pond: Seasholes 2003, 92; reanalysis: Laskowski 2011.

3. Revealing insights: Luiz 2014; prostitutes greatly valued personal hygiene: Luiz 2014.

4. Luiz 2014.

5. Luiz 2014.

6. Luiz 2014.

41. LOVE TOKEN

1. Seasholes 2003, 153.

2. Howe 1910, 60.

42. HORSE BLINDER

Opening photo by Jennifer Poulsen; courtesy of Miles Shugar.

1. Dalzell 1987, 3–4.

2. Warner 1978, 93.

3. River became polluted: Report of the City Engineer 1881; extensive archaeological investigations: Bower and Rushing 1979.

4. Guild and White Tannery: Bower et al. 1987; over 1,000 tons of bark: Bower et al. 1987.

5. Vats of molten iron: Bower and Charles 1988; at its peak: Bower and Charles 1988; archaeologists found: Bower and Charles 1988.

6. Metropolitan Horse Railroad: Bower et al. 1986; these excavations revealed: Shugar 2014, 283; when the railway was making the transition: Shugar 2014.

43. ROCK AND TAR BOTTLE

1. Laws were passed: Bridenbaug 1955, 239; public nuisance: Cheek and Balicki 2000, 59.

2. Elia 1997.

3. Poulsen 2011.

4. Landon 2007, 104.

44. HEBREW PRAYER BOOK

1. Seidenberg, n.d.

2. Jews have been present: Sarna et al. 1995, 5; new wave of East European Jewish immigrants: Sarna et al. 1995, 6.

45. LADY'S WALLET

1. Poulsen 2011.

2. Refuse deposited in Great Pond: Poulsen 2011; contents of the pond fill: Poulsen 2011.

3. Levenstein 1983.

46. COMB

1. Finkelman 2006, 48.

2. O'Day 1998.

3. Elia 1997.

47. RED SOX PIN

1. Riess 2006, 500.

2. Baseball diamond: Riess 2006, 500; first modern World Series: Abrams 2005; game series: Abrams 2005.

3. Riess 2006, 502.

4. Ritchie and Miller 1994.

50. SHOWTIME TOKEN

1. Giorlandino 1986, 10.

2. Giorlandino 1986, 12.

3. Combat Zone: Giorlandino 1986, 14; dramatic rise: Giorlandino 1986, 19; BRA . . . devised: Giorlandino 1986, 29; redesignation: Giorlandino 1986, 29.

4. Giorlandino 1986, 81.

5. Giorlandino 1986, 39–40.

6. Eroded the economic stability: Giorlandino 1986, 45; Raymond Flynn: Giorlandino 1986, 47; eviction and redevelopment: Giorlandino 1986, 49.

Bibliography

Abdalian, Leon H.

1920   Temple Israel Jewish Synagogue, 602
    Commonwealth Avenue. Boston Public Library,
    Print Department (Abdalian identifier no. 2038),
    Boston Public Library, Boston, MA.

Aberdeen, Harry G.

1936 (ca.)   Pewter Mug, graphite on paper. National
    Gallery of Art, 1943.8.16936, Washington, DC.

Abrams, Roger I.

2005   *The First World Series and the Baseball
    Fanatics of 1903*. University Press of New England,
    Lebanon, NH.

Andrew, John

1850 (ca.)   Nathaniel Hawthorne. Ballou's Pictorial
    Drawing-room Companion.

Bacon, Edwin Monroe (editor)

1892   *Boston of To-Day: A Glance at Its History and
    Characteristics. With Biographical Sketches and
    Portraits of Many of Its Professional and Business
    Men.* Post Publishing Company, Boston, MA.

Barber, Samuel

1916   *Boston Common: A Diary of Notable
    Events, Incidents, and Neighboring Occurrences.*
    Christopher Publishing House, Boston, MA.

Blitz, John H.

1988   Adoption of the Bow in Prehistoric North
    America. *North American Archaeologist* 9(2):123–
    145.

Bond, Edmunds E.

1914   *Fenway Park, 1914 World Series.* Boston
    Public Library, Prints Department, Boston, MA.

Bonner, John

1722   1722. *[Map of] The Town of Boston in New
    England.* Norman B. Leventhal Map Center,
    Boston Public Library. < http://maps.bpl.org
    /id/11122>. Accessed 20 April 2015.

Boston (City of)

1972   *African Meeting House.* City of Boston
    Archives, Boston Landmarks Commission image
    collection, 5210.004, Boston, MA.

1860   *Boston Common.* Print. Boston Public Library,
    Prints Department, Box: Parks; Boston Common
    (prints), Boston, MA.

1867   *Boston Harbor, Massachusetts, United States
    Coast Survey.* Norman B. Leventhal Map Center
    at the Boston Public Library. <Maps.bpl.org
    /id/12066>. Accessed 26 April 2015.

1992   *City Square Historical and Archaeological Site.*
    Boston Landmarks Commission, Boston, MA.

1915.   *Dor. Tun. Houses #18–20 Dexter St.* Boston
    Public Library Prints department, Boston, MA.

1868–1902 (ca.)   *Mt. Hope Home.* Boston Public
    Library, Print Department, Boston North End
    Mission Photographs, Boston, MA.

1857   *Open Car of the Metropolitan Horse Railroad,
    Passing the Winthrop House, Boston.* Boston Public
    Library, Print Department, R. R. & Subways:
    Miscellaneous, Boston, MA.

1815   *A View on Boston Common.* Boston Public
    Library, Prints Department, Parks: Boston
    Common (Prints), Boston, MA.

1868–1902 (ca.)   *A Window Pull.* Boston Public
    Library, Print Department, Boston North End
    Mission Photographs, Boston, MA.

Boston (Mass.) Engineering Department

1881   Report of the City Engineer

Boston Redevelopment Authority

Boston Town Records

1646   Record Commissioners, May 18.

Boston Town Records

1660–1701   Record Commissioners, 7:33.

Boston Transit Commission

1905   *Building on Washington Street between Brattle Street and Cornhill.* City of Boston Archives, Public Works Department photograph collection, 5000.009, Boston, MA.

Bower, Beth Anne

1986   The African Meeting House Boston, Massachusetts Summary Report of Archaeological Excavations 1975–1986. Report at the Massachusetts Historical Commission, Boston.

Bower, Beth, and Byron Rushing

1979   Archaeological Reconnaissance Survey of the Southwest Corridor Project Area. Report at the Massachusetts Historical Commission, Boston.

Bower, Beth Anne, Sheila Charles, and John Cheney

1987   The Guild and White Company Tannery Site, Roxbury, Massachusetts: Report on the Phase III Archaeological Data Recovery. Report at the Massachusetts Historical Commission, Boston.

Bower, Beth Anne, and Sheila Charles

1988   The Highland Foundry Site, Roxbury, Massachusetts. Report on Phase III Archaeological Data Recovery. Report at the Massachusetts Historical Commission, Boston.

Bower, Beth Anne, Sheila Charles, Constance Crosby, and Woodard Openo

1986   Massachusetts Bay Transportation Authority Southwest Corridor Project. The Metropolitan Railroad Company Complex Site at Roxbury Crossing, Roxbury. Report at the Massachusetts Historical Commission, Boston.

Bowditch, N. I.

1827–1859   Bowditch collection of Boston conveyances, Massachusetts Historical Society papers, Boston.

Bradley, James W. Arthur J. Krim, Peter Stott, Sarah Zimmerman, and James W. Bradley

1982   Historical and Archaeological Resources of the Boston Area: A Framework for Preservation Decision. Report at the Massachusetts Historical Commission, Boston.

Bremser, Johann G.

1822   *Traité zoologique et physiologique sur les vers* *intestinaux de l'homme.* C. L. F. Panckoucke, editor, Imprimerie de C. L. F. Panckoucke, Paris.

Bridenbaug, Carl

1955   *Cities in the Wilderness.* Alfred A. Knopf, New York, NY.

British Parliament

1765   *The Stamp Act.*

Browman, David L., and Stephen Williams

2013   *Anthropology at Harvard: A Biographical History, 1790–1940.* Peabody Museum Monographs, 11, Harvard University Press, Cambridge MA.

Bruce, George Anson

1906   *The Twentieth Regiment of Massachusetts Volunteer Infantry, 1861–1865.* Houghton Mifflin, New York, NY.

Burgis, William

1728   *To His Excellency William Burnet, Esqr. This Plan of Boston in New England Is Humbly Dedicated.* Norman B. Leventhal Map Center at the Boston Public Library. <Maps.bpl.org /id/10063>. Accessed 27 May 2015.

Byron, R.

1750–1799 (ca.)   *View of the South End of Boston in New England American & of the Neck Taken from the Hill N. E. of the Common.* Boston Public Library, Print Department, Box: General Views: Boston before 1800, Boston, MA.

Carr, Jacqueline Barbara

2005   *After the Siege: A Social History of Boston, 1775–1800.* University Press of New England, Lebanon, NH.

Cassedy, Daniel, Kimberly Morrell, Thomas Kutys, Matt Jorgenson, and Edward Morin

2013   Archaeological Investigations in Support of the Transportation and Information Hub Project, Faneuil Hall, Boston, Massachusetts, Archaeological Data Recovery Report. Report at the Massachusetts Historical Commission, Boston.

Cheek, Charles D., and Joseph Balicki

2000   Volume 1, Technical Report, Archaeological Data Recovery, the Mill Pond Site (Bos-HA-14),

Boston, Massachusetts. Report at the
Massachusetts Historical Commission, Boston.

Clapp, Edwin Jones

1916 *The Port of Boston: A Study and a Solution of
the Traffic and Operating Problems of Boston, and
Its Place in the Competition of the North Atlantic
Seaports.* Yale University Press, New Haven, CT.

Clements, Joyce M.

1993 The Cultural Creation of the Feminine
Gender: An Example from 19th-Century
Military Households at Fort Independence,
Boston. *Historical Archaeology* 27(4):39–64.

Colonial Laws of Massachusetts

1651 Sumptuary Laws (Laws Regarding What One
May or May Not Wear).

Cook, Lauren J., and Joseph Balicki

1998 Archaeological Data Recovery: The
Paddy's Alley and Cross Street Back Lot Sites
(BOS-HA-12/13), Boston, Massachusetts. Report
at the Massachusetts Historical Commission,
Boston.

Cook, Lauren J.

1998 "Katherine Nanny, Alias Naylor": A Life in
Puritan Boston. *Historical Archaeology* 32(1):15–19.

Cox, Christopher

2013 History of Massachusetts Civil War
Regiments: Artillery, Cavalry, and Infantry. <Lulu.
com>. Accessed 28 May 2015.

Creative-museum

2010 *Comb Made of Tortoise Shell.* Wiki Commons.
<Commons.wikimedia.org>. Accessed 19
September 2015.

Culpeper, Nicholas

1992 *Culpeper's Color Herbal.* Sterling, New York,
NY.

Currier, Nathaniel

1846 *The Destruction of Tea at Boston Harbor.*
Wiki Commons. <Commons.wikimedia.org>.
Accessed 27 April 2015.

Curtis and Cameron

1808–1812 (ca.) *State House from Common. 1812.*
Boston Public Library, Print Department, Box:
Parks: Boston Common (prints), Boston, MA.

Dalzell, Robert F.

1987 *Enterprising Elite: The Boston Associates and
the World They Made.* No. 40. Harvard University
Press, Cambridge, MA.

Decima, Elena B., and Dena F. Dincauze

1998 The Boston Back Bay Fish Weirs. In *Hidden
Dimensions: The Cultural Significance of Wetland
Archaeology,* Kathryn Bernick, editor, pp. 157–172.
University of Washington Press, Seattle.

Delano, Sterling F.

2009 *Brook Farm.* Harvard University Press,
Cambridge, MA.

Des Barres, Joseph F. W.

1775 *A Chart of the Harbour of Boston.* Normal
B. Leventhal Map Center at the Boston Public
Library. <Maps.bpl.org/id/10104>. Accessed 28
March 2015.

Diderot, Denis

1771 *Encyclopédie, ou dictionnaire raisonné des
sciences, des arts, et des métiers.* Plates, Vol. 8. Chez
Briasson, Paris.

Dincauze, Dena F.

1968 Preliminary Report on the Charles
River Archaeological Survey. Report at the
Massachusetts Historical Commission, Boston.

Donta, Christopher

2006 The Neponset Paleoindian Site (19-NF-70)
in Canton, Massachusetts: Archaeological Data
Recovery Surveys 2002–2003. Report at the
Massachusetts Historical Commission, Boston.

Dooley-Fairchild, Sira

2014 Discussion with Joseph Bagley, City
Archaeology Laboratory, Boston, MA, 5 June
2014.

Doucette, Dianna L., and John R. Cross

1997 Annasnappet Pond Archaeological District:
An Archaeological Data Recovery Program,
North Carver, Massachusetts. Report at the
Massachusetts Historical Commission, Boston.

Duis, Perry

1999 *The Saloon: Public Drinking in Chicago and
Boston, 1880–1920.* University of Illinois Press,
Urbana.

Edens, Christopher M., and Robert G. Kingsley

1998   The Spectacle Island Site: Middle to Late Woodland Adaptations in Boston Harbor, Suffolk County, Massachusetts, Central Artery/Tunnel Project, Boston Massachusetts. Report at the Massachusetts Historical Commission, Boston.

Edes, Henry

1880   Charlestown in the Provential Period. In *The Memorial History of Boston*, Justin Winsor, editor, pp. 547–562. James Osgood, Boston, MA.

Edmonson, Ellen, and Hugh Chrisp

1927–1940   *New York Biological Survey.* Conservation Department, New York State.

Elia, Ricardo J., David B. Landon, and Nancy S. Seasholes

1989   Phase II Archaeological Investigations of the Central Artery/Third Harbor Tunnel Project in Boston, Massachusetts. Report at the Massachusetts Historical Commission, Boston.

Elia, Ricardo J.

1997   Archaeological Investigations at the Paul Revere House in Boston, Massachusetts. Report at the Massachusetts Historical Commission, Boston.

Emilio, Luis Fenollosa

1894   *History of the Fifty-Fourth Regiment of Massachusetts Volunteer Infantry, 1863–1865.* Boston Book Company, Boston, MA.

Fairchild Aerial Surveys, Inc.

1925   *Boston. Harbor. Fort Independence, Castle Is.* Boston Public Library, Print Department, Fairchild Aerial Photos, South Boston and East Boston, Boston, MA.

Farrell, Betty

1993   *Elite Families: Class and Power in Nineteenth-Century Boston.* State University of New York Press, Albany.

Finkelman, Paul (editor)

2006   *Encyclopedia of African American History, 1619–1895: From the Colonial Period to the Age of Frederick Douglass, Three-Volume Set.* Vol. 3. Oxford University Press, New York, NY.

Fiske, John

1898   *The Beginnings of New England; or, The Puritan Theocracy in Its Relations to Civil and Religious Liberty.* Houghton Mifflin, New York, NY.

Folsom, Augustine H.

1892   *Paul Revere School. Grade 2.* Boston Public Library, Print Department, Boston Public Schools: Volume: Primary & Lower Grammar Classes, 1st to 5th Years, 1892: Photos by A. H. Folsom, Boston, MA.

Fowler, William S.

1966   Ceremonial and Domestic Products of Aboriginal New England. *Bulletin of the Massachusetts Archaeological Society* 27(3/4):33–68.

Fraquelin, Jean Baptiste Louis

1693   *Carte de la ville, baye et environs de Baston.* Norman B. Leventhal Map Center at the Boston Public Library. <http://maps.bpl.org/id/10918>. Accessed 26 May 2015.

Freake-Gibbs (attrib.)

1670 (ca.)   *David, Joanna, and Abigail Mason.* Fine Arts Museums of San Francisco, gift of Mr. and Mrs. John. D. Rockefeller III. 1979.7.3.

Frothingham, Richard

1890   *History of the Siege of Boston: And of the Battles of Lexington, Concord, and Bunker Hill: Also an Account of the Bunker Hill Monument.* Little, Brown, New York, NY.

Gallagher, Joan, Laurie Boros, Neill DePaoli, K. Ann Turner, and Joyce Fitzgerald

1994   Archaeological Data Recovery, City Square Archaeological District, Central Artery North Reconstruction Project, Charlestown, Massachusetts. Volume 7. Report at the Massachusetts Historical Commission, Boston.

Gallagher, Joan, Laurie Boros, Joyce Fitzgerald, and Neill DePaoli

1992   The Parker-Harris Pottery Site, Central Artery North Reconstruction Project, Archaeological Data Recovery, Charlestown, Massachusetts. Volume 3. Report at the Massachusetts Historical Commission, Boston.

Gies and Company

1870–1900 (ca.)   *What Are the Babies After? Lactated Food.* Buffalo, N.Y. Boston Public Library, Print Department, advertising cards; cut-paper works, Boston, MA.

Giorlandino, Salvatore S.

1986   The Origin, Development, and Decline of Boston's Adult Entertainment District: The Combat Zone. Master's thesis, City Planning, Massachusetts Institute of Technology, Cambridge.

Grant, Spencer

1974   *Adult Movie Theatres, Combat Zone.* Boston Public Library, Print Department, Spencer Grant Collection, Boston, MA.

1974   *Transvestite Stage Show, Combat Zone.* Boston Public Library, Print Department, Spencer Grant Collection, Boston, MA.

Grimes, John R., William Eldridge, Beth G. Grimes, Antonio Vaccaro, Frank Vaccaro, Joseph Vaccaro, Nicolas Vaccaro, and Antonio Orsini

1984   Bull Brook II. *Archaeology of Eastern North America* 12:159–183.

Hickey, Donald R.

1989   *The War of 1812.* University of Illinois Press, Urbana, IL.

Homer, Winslow

1858.   The Boston Common. *Harper's Weekly* 2(2):329.

Hooton, Earnest A.

1943   Charles Clark Willoughby, 1857–1943. *American Antiquity* 9(2):235–239.

Howe, Mark Antony De Wolfe

1910   *Boston Common: Scenes from Four Centuries.* Houghton Mifflin, Boston, MA.

Hughes, Thomas P.

1957   *Medicine in Virginia, 1607–1699.* Virginia 350th Anniversary Celebration Corporation, Williamsburg, VA.

Hull, Charles

1992   *Pewter.* Osprey Publishing, London.

Hunnewell, James A.

1915   *Very Old Corner of Boston.* Bostonian Society Publications, 2. Boston, MA.

Ion, Hamish

2010   *American Missionaries, Christian Oyatoi, and Japan, 1859–73.* University of British Columbia Press, Vancouver.

Jaynes, Gerald D. (editor)

2005   *Encyclopedia of African American Society.* Sage Publications, Thousand Oaks, CA.

Jefferson, Thomas

1784   *Notes on the Establishment of a Money Unit, and of a Coinage for the United States April, 1784.*

Johnson, Frederick

1942   *The Boylston Street Fishweir.* Robert S. Peabody Foundation for Archaeology, Andover, MA.

Jones, Leslie

1939–1945 (ca.)   *WWII.* Boston Public Library, Print Department, Leslie Jones Collection, Boston, MA.

1940–1949   *Trinity Church, Copley Square, Showing Victory Garden.* Boston Public Library, Print Department, Leslie Jones Collection, Boston, MA.

1950–1959 (ca.)   *Civil War Monument in Charlestown, "Training Field" near Monument Square, Winthrop St., etc.,* Boston Public Library, Leslie Jones Collection, Boston, MA.

1956   *Young Red Sox Fans at Fenway for Opening Day.* Boston Public Library, Prints Department, Leslie Jones Collection, Boston, MA.

Landon, David B.

1996   Feeding Colonial Boston: A Zooarchaeological Study. *Historical Archaeology* 30(1):1–153.

2007   Investigating the Heart of a Community: Archaeological Excavations at the African Meeting House, Boston, Massachusetts. Report at the Massachusetts Historical Commission, Boston.

Laskowski, Amy

2011   Revelations of a Brothel's Trash, CAS Archaeology Team Studies 19th-Century Medicines, Syringes, and Tooth Powder. *Bostonia,* Summer. Boston University, Boston, MA.

Levenstein, Harvey

1983   "Best for Babies" or "Preventable Infanticide"? The Controversy over Artificial Feeding of Infants in America, 1880–1920. *Journal of American History* 70(1):75–94.

Library of Congress, U.S. Congressional Documents and Debates

1807   1774–1875, 2 Stat. 451.

Lothrop, Jonathan C., Paige E. Newby, Arthur E. Spiess, and James W. Bradley

2011   Paleoindians and the Younger Dryas in the New England–Maritimes Region. *Quaternary International* 242(2):546–569.

Luedtke, Barbara

1975   Final Report on the Archaeological and Paleobotanical Resources on Twelve Islands in Boston Harbor. Report at the Massachusetts Historical Commission, Boston.

Luiz, Jade

2014   Under the Corset: Health, Hygiene, and Maternity in Boston's North End. Paper presented at the Society for Historical Archaeology annual conference, Quebec City, Quebec, Canada.

Lyman, Theodore

1823   *A Short Account of the Hartford Convention: Taken from Official Documents, and Addressed to the Fair Minded and the Well Disposed: To Which Is Added an Attested Copy of the Secret Journal of That Body.* No. 63537. O. Everett, Boston, MA.

MacGregor, Neil

2011   *A History of the World in 100 Objects.* Penguin, London, UK.

Marr, Thomas E.

1909   *Boston Slums, 1909.* Boston Public Library, Print Department, Neighborhoods; North End: Misc., Boston, MA.

Massachusetts Historical Society

1918   Proceedings of the Massachusetts Historical Society, Volume 51. Massachusetts Historical Society, Boston, Massachusetts.

Mather, Cotton

2009   *Magnalia Christi Americana.* Vol. 2. Applewood Books, Bedford, MA.

McFarland, Philip

2004   *Hawthorne in Concord.* Grove Press, New York, NY.

Merrifield, Ralph

1988   *The Archaeology of Ritual and Magic.* New Amsterdam Books, New York, NY.

Mills, Joel

2013   *Whipworm Egg Crop.* Image published under Creative Commons Attribute—Share Alike 2.5, 2.0, and 1.0, generic license. Wiki Commons. <http://commons.wikimedia.org/wiki/File:Whipworm_egg_crop.JPG>. Accessed 28 May 2015.

Moore, Jacob Bailey

1848   *Lives of the Governors of New Plymouth, and Massachusetts Bay.* Gates & Stedman, Boston, MA.

Mrozowski, Stephen A.

1985   *Boston's Archaeological Legacy: The City's Planning and Policy Document.* Boston Landmarks Commission, Boston, MA.

Mumcuoglu, Kosta Y.

2008   The Louse Comb: Past and Present. *American Entomologist* 54(3):164–166.

Museum of Fine Arts

1916   *Bulletin* 14(86).

National Gallery (Washington, D.C.)

1783 (ca.)   *American Attack on Bunker's Hill, with the Burning of Charles Town.* National Gallery of Art, Gift of Edgar William and Bernice Crysler Garbisch, 1953.5.86, Washington, DC.

Neumann, George C., and Frank J. Kravic

1975   *Collector's Illustrated Encyclopedia of the American Revolution.* Stackpole Books, Mechanicsburg, PA.

Noel Hume, Ivorz

2001   *A Guide to the Artifacts of Colonial America.* University of Pennsylvania Press, Philadelphia.

O'Day, Alan

1998   *Irish Home Rule, 1867–1921.* Manchester University Press, Manchester, UK.

O. H. Bailey and Company

1888   *Boston Highlands, Massachusetts, Wards 19, 20, 21, & 22.* Norman B. Leventhal Map Center at the Boston Public Library. <Maps.bpl.org/id/10156>. Accessed 28 May 2015.

Page, Thomas H.

1777   *A Plan of the Town of Boston with the Entrenchments of His Majesty's Forces in 1775; from the Observations of Lieut. Page of His Majesty's Corps of Engineers, and from Those of Other Gentlemen.* Leventhal Map Center at the Boston Public Library. <Maps.bpl.org/id/n50904>. Accessed 27 April 2015.

1793   *A Plan of the Action at Bunker's Hill, on the 17th of June 1775.* Leventhal Map Center at the Boston Public Library. <Maps.bpl.org/id/10037>. Accessed 27 April 2015.

Pendery, Steven R.

1988   Archaeological Survey of the Boston Common, Boston, Massachusetts. Report at the Massachusetts Historical Commission, Boston.

1992   Consumer Behavior in Colonial Charlestown, Massachusetts, 1630–1760. *Historical Archaeology* 26(3):57–72.

Pendery, Steven R., Russell Barber, Peter Bogucki, Penelope Lie, and David Singer

1984   Phase III, Chelsea–Water Streets Connector Project, Charlestown, Massachusetts: Excavations at the Wapping Street and Maudlin Street Archaeological Districts. Report at the Massachusetts Historical Commission, Boston.

Plymouth Ancestors

2010 (ca.)   Raising Children in the Early 17th Century: Demographics. Plimoth Plantation and New England Historical Genealogical Society. Plymouth, MA.

Poulsen, Jennifer

2011   *Urban Consumption in Late 19th-Century Dorchester.* Master's thesis, Department of Anthropology, University of Massachusetts–Boston, University Microfilms International, Ann Arbor, MI.

Quint, A. H.

1879   Notes on the Dover (N.H.) Combination of 1640. *New England Historical and Genealogical Register* 33:91–101.

Revere, Paul

1768   *A View of the Town of Boston in New England and British Ships of War Landing Their Troops, 1768.* Boston Public Library, Print Department, Cab 23.58.1, Boston, MA.

Riess, Steven A.

2006   *Encyclopedia of Major League Baseball Clubs.* Greenwood, Santa Barbara, CA.

Ritchie, Duncan, Joan Gallagher and Barbara Luedtke

1984   An Intensive-Level Archaeological Survey on Deer and Long Islands, Boston Harbor, Massachusetts. Report at the Massachusetts Historical Commission, Boston.

Ritchie, Duncan, and Beth P. Miller

1994   Archaeological Investigations of the Prehistoric and Historic Period Components of the Dillaway-Thomas House Site, Roxbury Heritage State Park, Boston, Massachusetts. Report at the Massachusetts Historical Commission, Boston.

Roberts, Oliver Ayer

1895   *History of the Military Company of the Massachusetts, Now Called the Ancient and Honorable Artillery Company of Massachusetts: 1637–1888. Vol. 1.* A. Mudge and Son, Boston, MA.

Sarna, Jonathan D., Ellen Smith, and Scott-Martin Kosofsky

1995   *The Jews of Boston.* Combined Jewish Philanthropies of Greater Boston, Boston, MA.

Savage, Edward Hartwell

1873   *Police Records and Recollections; or, Boston by Daylight and Gaslight: For Two Hundred and Forty Years.* J. P. Dale, Boston, MA.

Schouler, William

1868   *A History of Massachusetts in the Civil War. Vol. 1.* E. P. Dutton, Boston, MA.

Seasholes, Nancy S.

2003   *Gaining Ground: A History of Landmaking in Boston.* MIT Press, Cambridge, MA.

Secretary of the Commonwealth of Massachusetts

1841–1891   Passenger Manifest Lists, Secretary of the Commonwealth of Massachusetts.

Seidenberg, David R.

[300–500?]   *Sanctification of the Moon, Kiddush*

Levanah. Open Siddur Project. <Opensiddur.org>. Accessed 30 April 2015.

Shammas, Carole
1994   Re-Assessing the Married Women's Property Acts. *Journal of Women's History* 6(1):9–30.

Shaw, Robert G.
1861   Letter from Robert Gould Shaw to Francis George Shaw, 19 May. MS Am 1910 (38), Houghton Library, Harvard University, Cambridge, MA.

Shipton, Clifford Kenyon
1960   *Biographical Sketches of Those Who Attended Harvard College in the Classes of 1741–1745; with Bibliographical and Other Notes.* Massachusetts Historical Society, Boston.

Shugar, Miles
2014   From Horse to Electric Power at the Metropolitan Railroad Company Site: Archaeology and the Narrative of Technological Change. Master's thesis, Anthropology Department, University of Massachusetts–Boston.

Skehan, James
2001   *Roadside Geology of Massachusetts.* Mountain Press Publishing Company, Missoula, MT.

Smith, Frederick M.
1870–1879 (ca.)   *Commonwealth Avenue, North Side.* Boston Public Library, Prints Department, Street Views: Commonwealth Ave., Boston, MA.

Smith, Sidney
1902   *A Prospective View of Part of the Commons.* Boston Public Library, Print Department, Oversized Photographs: Flat file, Boston, MA.

Stark, James Henry
1907   *The Loyalists of Massachusetts and the Other Side of the American Revolution.* W. B. Clarke, Boston.

Stokinger, William A., and Geoffrey P. Moran
1978   A Final Report of Archaeological Investigations at Fort Independence: 1976–1977. Volumes 1 and 2. Report at the Massachusetts Historical Commission, Boston.

Stone, Lyle M.
1974   *Fort Michilimackinac 1715–1781: An Archaeological Perspective on the Revolutionary Frontier.* Publications of the Museum, Michigan State University, East Lansing.

Sully, Thomas
1818   *Lady with Harp: Eliza Ridgely.* National Gallery of Art, Gift of Maude Monell Vetlesen, 1945.9.1, Washington, DC.

Suffolk County Probate Records
Suffolk County Probate Records, Massachusetts Archives, no. 348.
Suffolk County Probate Records, Massachusetts Archives, no. 3718.

Superior Court of Suffolk County
1671 (ca.)   Manuscript at the Massachusetts State Archives, Boston.

Ticknor, Caroline
1913   *Hawthorne and His Publisher.* Houghton Mifflin, New York, NY.

Ulrich, Laurel
1982   *Good Wives: Image and Reality in the Lives of Women in Northern New England, 1650–1750.* Vintage, New York, NY.

United Kingdom of Great Britain and Ireland
1812   An Act Declaring War between the United Kingdom of Great Britain and Ireland and the Dependencies thereof and the United States of America and Their Territories Approved June 18, 1812.

United States Coast Survey

Vanderlyn, Pieter
1730   *Susanna Traux.* National Gallery of Art. Gift of Edgar William and Bernice Chrysler Garbisch, 1980.62.31, Washington DC.

Walsh, Joseph M.
1892   *Tea, Its History and Mystery.* Privately published.

Ward, Gerald W. R.
2001   *New England Silver and Silversmithing, 1620–1815.* Colonial Society of Massachusetts, Boston, MA.

Warner, Sam Bass
1978   *Streetcar Suburbs.* Harvard University Press, Cambridge, MA.

Whipple, John Adams

1859–1870 (ca.) *Robt G. Shaw*. Boston Public
    Library, Print Department, Boston, MA.

Whitney, Charles

1843 *Map of the Town of Roxbury, Surveyed
    by Order of the Town Authorities*. Norman B.
    Leventhal Map Center, Boston Public Library.
    <Maps.bpl.org/id/14925>. Accessed 23 May 2015.

Wilder, Burt Green

1875 *Sketch of Dr. Jeffries Wyman*. Publisher not
    identified.

Wilson, James G., and John Fiske

1889 *Appletons' Cyclopedia of American Biography,
    Volume 6*. D. Appleton, New York, NY.

Wood, William

1993 *New England's Prospect*. University of
    Massachusetts Press, Amherst.

Wyman, Thomas Bellows

1879 *The Genealogies and Estates of Charlestown
    in the County of Middlesex and Commonwealth
    of Massachusetts, 1629–1818*. D. Clapp and Son,
    Boston, MA.

Index

Page numbers in *italics* refer to the illustrations.

Canton (now Guangzhou), 82

carbon-14 dating, 17, 26

Carnes, John, 91–92. *See also* John Carnes site, North End

Carver, 14

Castle Island, 11, *125*

catering services, 129

cat skeleton, Three Cranes Tavern, 75, *75–77, 76,* 182n21

Central Artery/Tunnel project (Big Dig), 3–4, 5, 38, 40, 43, 46, 56, 73, 86, 88, 91, 111, 141, 178

ceramics. *See* pottery

chamber pots: Katherine Nanny Naylor Privy, *42,* 42–44, 181n11; Parker-Harris style, found at Three Cranes Tavern site, *88,* 182n25

Champlain, Samuel de, 34

Charles I (king of England), 37

Charles II (king of England), 99

Charles River Basin, 2, 11, 21

Charlestown: Big Dig and, 3; burning and rebuilding of, 83, 85, 102, 107–8, *110,* 110–11; Civil War monument, training field, *138;* foundation of, 31, 34, 37–38; Garrett site pottery, 39, *39–41, 41;* Great House, City Square, stone from, 36, *36–38, 38,* 181n9; map, *40;* Naylor, Katherine Nanny, moving to, 57; in Revolutionary War, 102, *107,* 107–8. *See also* City Square; Parker-Harris pottery site, Charleston; Three Cranes Tavern, City Square

Charlestown Navy Yard, 176

Charlotte (queen of England), 98

Chatham, fluted point from, *11,* 181n1

cherry bounce/cherry wine, 63

children: Clough House, toys found in, *169;* in colonial Boston, *49, 59–60,* 71, 78, 79–80; cop and robber cast-lead figures, Brook Farm, *168,* 171, 183n48; education of, 136, *163,* 164; gender roles and, 60, 169–71; orphanages, *170,* 171; in postrevolutionary Boston, 146, 160, 163, 164, *166, 167,* 169–71; school bell dome, Brook Farm, *168,* 171, 183n48; shoe, child's, Katherine Nanny Naylor privy, *58,* 58–60, *60,* 181n16; whizzer, Faneuil Hall, *78,* 78–80, 182n22

China: direct trade between Boston and, 118; pottery imported from, 40, 82, 83; tea drinking imported from, 99

City Archaeology Laboratory, 3, 5, 18, 26

City Archaeology Program, xi–xii, 3–6, 179

City Square: bar shot, 106, *106–8,* 182n30; cannonball, British, 107, *108,* 182n30; Charlestown, foundation of, 31, 37–38; Great House, stone from, 36, *36–38, 38,* 181n9. *See also* Three Cranes Tavern, City Square

Civil War (British), 40

Civil War (US): Boston and Massachusetts citizens in, 138–39; monument, training field, Charlestown, *138;* New York militia button, Brook Farm, *137,* 137–39, *139,* 183n39

class distinctions in Boston, 60, 65, 68, 79, 115, 116, 145–46

clay tobacco pipes: from Garrett site, Charlestown, 41; from John Carnes site, North End, *70,* 70–72, *71,* 182n20

clothing. *See* textiles and clothing

Clough House, North End: children's toys from, *169;* gaming token from, 79, 182n22; lipstick, *172,* 172–74, *173,* 183n49; from single-family home to tenement, 144

coinage and mints, US, *117,* 117–19, *118*

Collins, John, 177

colonial/Puritan era (1629–1700), 3, 6, 31. *See also specific sites and artifacts*

colonoware fragment, Katherine Nanny Naylor privy, 72, 182n20

"Combat Zone," *176,* 176–78, *177*

combs: Bakelite comb, Paul Revere House, North End, *161,* 161–64, 183n46; lice comb, Katherine Nanny Naylor privy, 47, 181n12; tortoiseshell comb, Boston Common, *124,* 124–27, *127,* 183n35

Commonwealth Avenue, 144, 145, 156

Concord and Lexington, Battles of, 101–2, 107

USS *Constitution,* 40

Constitutional Convention (1787), 118

copaiba oil bottle, Endicott Street privy, North End, *142,* 183n40

cop and robber cast-lead figures, Brook Farm, West Roxbury, *168,* 169–71, 183n48